Preface

With the ICT infrastructure gaining significant development in the past decade, the growing sophistication of e-Government in developing countries has effectively contributed to the e-participation of women and the achievement of the UN Millennium Development Goals. Gender mainstreaming in ICT policies, particularly through e-government initiatives, has been placed at the top of development agenda in recent years, and the Beijing Declaration and Platform for Action and the Millennium Development Goals have both encouraged governments to adopt a gender-perspective and to enhance women's rights in public policies.

The Asia-Pacific Regional MDG Report 2012/13 highlighted an abiding bias against women, despite significant progress in other areas and noted that "women continue to face severe deficits in health and education and in their access to power, voice and rights". Women are also more likely than men to be in vulnerable employment, with 52% of women in vulnerable employment in East Asia, 65.6% in South-East Asia and the Pacific and 83.3% in South Asia (ILO Global Employment Trends for Women, 2012). Globally, Asia and the Pacific have the world's second-lowest percentage of women parliamentarians. Whether in public or private sphere, from highest levels of government decision-making to households, women continue to be denied equal opportunity with men to participate in decisions that affect their lives.

With the concern on how to utilize e-government as an effective policy tool to promote gender equality and empower women, the United Nations Project Office on Governance (UNPOG) initiated and launched the research project in September 2011 on the role of e-Government from promoting gender equality to empowering women in Asia and the Pacific. The Phase I research conducted in 2011, categorized the varied levels of e-government development in the region and presented an analytical framework to measure and evaluate how e-Government development and the application of ICT tools have contributed to gender equality in six selected countries, namely Bangladesh, Indonesia, Malaysia, Philippines, Republic of Korea and Viet Nam. The Phase I research provided valuable guidance on how these countries can further promote gender equality through gender mainstreaming ICT policies and e-government initiatives.

On 13 February 2012, UNPOG in collaboration with the Asia Pacific Women's Information Network Center (APWINC) organized an expert group meeting (EGM) with attendance of experts from UNDP, UN Women and UNESCAP and representatives from academia, NGOs and government institutions in the Republic of Korea to evaluate Phase I research proceedings. The EGM concluded with a positive assessment of the Phase I research outcome as well as a number of key recommendations on how to further develop the research particularly on expanding the number of countries to be surveyed. Thus, following the recommendations from the EGM and with the approval from the Division for Public Administration and Development Management, Department of Economic and Social Affairs (DESA), UNPOG conducted Phase II research in 2012 with expanded country coverage by including 5 additional countries, namely China, Fiji, India, Mongolia and Timor-Leste, together with the compilation and analysis of case studies in those countries.

The UNPOG project findings noted that gender initiatives should be incorporated in national ICT strategies and e-Government development policies, and proposed guidelines for governments on policy initiatives for developing a national action plan to promote gender equality through e-Government.

The success of the research should be attributed to the close collaboration with national experts for their support to fill out Surveys with good data quality, coupled with their reporting with most updated information for gauging the trends of gender equality versus ICT policies in selected countries. Special thanks should be bestowed on local research partners for their consistent support in conducting the surveys.

I believe that the report provides a good foundation for future research and is a good advocacy for a more gender-sensitive approach in ICT policy and e-Government development.

Jae-hong Lim
Head
United Nations Project Office on Governance
Division for Public Administration and Development Management
United Nations Department of Economic and Social Affairs
Seoul, January 2014

From Promoting Gender Equality to Empowering Women

The Role of e-Government in Asia and the Pacific

United Nations
2014

DESA

The Department of Economic and Social Affairs of the United Nations Secretariat is a vital interface between global policies in the economic, social and environmental spheres and national action. The Department works in three main interlinked areas: (i) it generates, compiles and analyzes a wide range of economic, social and environmental data and information on which Member States of the United Nations draw to review common problems and to take stock of policy options; (ii) it facilitates the negotiations of Member States in many intergovernmental bodies on joint courses of action to address ongoing or emerging global challenges; and (iii) it advises interested Governments on the ways and means of translating policy frameworks developed in United Nations conferences and summits into programmes at the country level and, through technical assistance, helps build national capacities.

Disclaimers

The designations employed and the presentations of the material in this publication do not imply the expression of any opinion whatsoever on the part of the Secretariat of the United Nations concerning the legal status of any country, territory, city or area, or of its authorities, concerning the delimitation of its frontiers or boundaries.

The designations "developed" and "developing economies" are intended for statistical convenience and do not necessarily imply a judgment about the stage reached by a particular country or area in the development process.

The views expressed are those of the individual authors and do not imply any expression of opinion on the part of the United Nations.

ST/ESA/SER.E/190
ISBN: 978-92-1-123201-1
e-ISBN: 978-92-1-056552-3
Sales No. E.14.II.H.3
Copyright © United Nations, 2014

Foreword

The adoption of ICT in the public sector has increasingly contributed to the inclusion of vulnerable groups including women in addressing development challenges, and a good number of governments in developing countries have fully endorsed e-Government initiatives to bridge the digital divide and promote gender equality and empower women.

In line with the Millennium Development Goals (MDG) Goal 3 to promote gender equality and empower women, e-Government can contribute, in full scale, to address gender inequality issues in education, labor market participation and equitable treatment, and participation in decision-making processes.

As part of the Post-2015 Development Agenda, governance norms must reflect principles of inclusion and participation, and promote transparent, accountable, capable institutions, at national and local levels, to realize national development goals and ensure a more dynamic, inclusive, equitable and sustainable development process with gender equality as one indispensable component in such governance norms.

Against this general background, the United Nations Project Office on Governance (UNPOG), a project office of the Division for Public Administration and Development Management, Department of Economic and Social Affairs (DESA), has conducted research in two phases (Phase I in 2011 and Phase II in 2012) on the role of e-government from promoting gender equality to empowering women in Asia and the Pacific.

The UNPOG research aimed to analyze the degree to which e-government development in Asia and the Pacific contribute to promote gender equality, provide a toolkit to assess national e-government readiness for gender equality and women's empowerment, and generate an e-government readiness index for gender equality.

The UNPOG research on the linkage between e-government and promoting gender equality is of unique value for promoting inclusive sustainable development especially in Asia and the Pacific.

It is hoped that this research by UNPOG can provide good references for governments in designing e-government policies and strategies.

Vincenzo Aquaro
Chief
E-Government Branch,
Division for Public Administration and Development Management
United Nations Department of Economic and Social Affairs
New York, January 2014

Acknowledgements

This publication is the result of the contributions and efforts of United Nations Project Office on Governance (UNPOG) in cooperation with experts from institutions dealing with gender and e-government issues.

The publication was prepared under the overall guidance of the late Haiyan Qian, Director of the Division for Public Administration and Development Management (DPADM) of the United Nations Department of Economic and Social Affairs (UNDESA) and Vincenzo Aquaro, Chief of e-Government Branch, DPADM, UNDESA. The publication benefited from the direction and overall supervision of Alexei Tikhomirov, Acting Head of United Nations Project Office on Governance (UNPOG). The UNPOG consultants Dong Ju Choi, Ph.D., Professor, Sookmyung Women's University and J. Hanah Zoo, Graduate School of International Studies, Yonsei University served as the principal authors of the publication who were supported with substantial and editorial inputs from Maud Ropars, Program Operations Expert, UNPOG; Vijay Parmar, Former Senior Governance and Public Administration Expert, UNPOG; HyunJung Kim, Associate Research & Policy Development Expert, UNPOG; and Sunyoung Chang, Former Associate Research & Policy Development Expert, UNPOG; and Emanuel Fabian, Research & Policy Development Intern, UNPOG. Special thanks are extended to Jonas Rabinovitch, Inter-Regional Advisor, DPADM, UNDESA and Valentina Resta, Governance and Public Administration Officer, DPADM, UNDESA for their substantive inputs, and Nathan Henninger, Communications, Publishing and Outreach, DPADM, UNDESA and Jina Kim, Associate Communications & Outreach Expert, UNPOG for their editorial assistance.

The survey, case study and web measurement analyses benefited from advice and guidance provided by following country experts and organizations: Sookhee Kwak, United Nations Development Programme (UNDP) Bangladesh; Shahana Siddiqui, UNDP Bangladesh; International Liaison Department, All China Women's Federation; Chen Lu, Yonsei University; Rajni Chand, Ph.D., University of the South Pacific Suva, Fiji; Rashpal Malhotra, Ph.D., Director, Center for Research in Rural & Industrial Development, India; Rila Mukherjee, Ph.D., Professor, University of Hyderabad, India; Yatty Maryati, Ministry of Women Empowerment and Child Protection, Indonesia; Siti Fatimah Khiriah M. Amin, Ministry of Women, Family and Community Development, Malaysia; Bekhtsetseg Tuvsanaa, Foreign Relations Officer, Information, Communications Technology and Post Authority of Mongolia; Battsetseg Enkhbaatar, National Committee on Gender Equality, Mongolia; Robert Matthew Romero, Head of ICT Unit, Philippine Commission on Women; Juli Ana E. Sudario, Deputy Managing Director, Information and Communications Technology Office, National Computer Center, Philippines; Ministry of Gender Equality and Family, Republic of Korea; Asia Pacific Women's Information Network Center, Sookmyung Women's University; Chungsoo Nam, Division of Research & Development, International Women and Family Foundation; Ki-Taek Jeon, Ph.D., Korean Women's Development Institute; Yoo-Jin Han, Ph.D., Assistant Professor, Sookmyung Women's University; YooRi Lee, Ph.D., Sookmyung Women's University; Haley Hyun, Sookmyung Women's University; Abel Pries da Silva, East Timor ICT Association, Timor-Leste; Insun Yu, Ph.D., Former Professor, Seoul National University; and Truong Thi Phuong Dung, Vietnam-Korea Friendship IT College, Viet Nam. Special contributors to the case studies include: Syeed Ahamed, Chief Executive Officer, Institute of Informatics and Development, Bangladesh; and Christian Wolff, Independent consultant, India.

Review is indebted to the following UN experts: Kilaparti Ramakrishna, Ph.D., Director of United Nations Economic and Social Commission for Asia and the Pacific (UNESCAP) Subregional Office for East and North-East Asia (SRO-ENEA); Yuko Kitada, Ph.D., Associate Social Affairs Officer, UNESCAP SRO-ENEA; Hyunju Shim, Consultant, UNESCAP SRO-ENEA; Julie Broussard, Country Programme Manager, UN Women China Office; Eunice Smith, Programme Specialist, UNESCO Office in Beijing.

Editorial supervision was provided by S. Revi Sterling, Ph.D., Faculty Director of ICTD graduate studies at ATLAS Institute, University of Colorado at Boulder, and Sonju Park, Sookmyung Women's University. Editorial assistance was provided by Jinyoung Park and Da-Gyum Ji.

Table of Contents

List of Figures

List of Tables

List of Boxes

Abbreviations and Acronyms

CICT	Commission on Information Communications Technology of Philippines
CITIGEN	Gender and Citizenship in the Information Society
COP	Community of Practice
CSC	Common Service Centre Initiative of India
DEIT	Department of Electronics and Information Technology of India
DPADM	Division for Public Administration and Development Management
e-AWEDAN	Electronic Application for Women Empowerment and Development Action by NGOs of India
EDF	European Development Fund
EGDI	E-Government Development Index
EGM	Expert Group Meeting
EU	European Union
G4C	Government for Citizens
G2B	Government to Business
G2C	Government to Citizen
G2E	Government to Employee
GenADRIS	Gender, Agriculture and Rural Development in the Information Society
GGGI	Global Gender Gap Index
GED	Gender Equality Department, MOLISA, Viet Nam
GII	Gender Inequality Index
GSIS	Gender Statistics Information System, Republic of Korea
GSMA	GSM Association
HDI	Human Development Index
HNPSP	Health, Nutrition and Population Sector Programme of Bangladesh
ICT	Information Communication Technology
ICTD	Information and Communication Technology for Development
ICTPA	Information and Communications Technology and Post Authority of Mongolia
IDI	ICT Development Index
IDRC	International Development Research Centre
IMAI	Internet and Mobile Association of India
ITU	International Telecommunication Union
KCC	Korea Communications Commission
MAMA	Mobile Alliance for Maternal Action
MDGs	Millennium Development Goals
MOG	Ministry of Gender of Republic of Korea
MOGEF	Ministry of Gender Equality and Family of Republic of Korea
MOLISA	Ministry of Labor-Invalids and Social Affairs of Viet Nam
MOCST	Ministry of Culture, Sport and Tourism of Viet Nam
MOSICT	Ministry of Science and Information and Communication Technology of Bangladesh
MOWCA	Ministry of Women and Child Affairs of Bangladesh
MWCSW	Ministry of Women, Culture and Social Welfare of Fiji
MWCD	Ministry of Women and Child Development of India
MWECP	Ministry of Women Empowerment and Child Protection of Indonesia
MWFCD	Ministry of Women, Family and Child Development of Malaysia
NCAW	National Committee for the Advancement of Women of Viet Nam
NCGE	National Committee on Gender Equality of Mongolia
NCW	National Commission for Women of India
NGO	Non-Governmental Organization

NIPA	National IT Industry Promotion Agency of Korea
NRI	Networked Readiness Index
NWCCW	National Working Committee on Children and Women of People's Republic of China
NZAID	New Zealand Agency for International Development
PCW	Philippine Commission on Women
RDSSED	Roadmap for Democracy & Sustainable Socio-Economic Development, Fiji
SKMM	Suruhanjaya Kmomunikasi Dan Multimedia Malaysia
SME	Small and Medium-sized Enterprise
SNS	Social Networking Service
SSPE	Secretary of State for the Promotion of Equality of Timor-Leste
UNDESA	United Nations Department of Economic and Social Affairs
UNDP	United Nations Development Programme
UNPAN	United Nations Online Network in Public Administration and Finance
UNPOG	United Nations Project Office on Governance
USAID	United States Agency for International Development
VWU	Viet Nam Women's Union
WEF	World Economic Forum
WICT4D	Women and Information Technologies for International Development

Executive Summary

The adoption of ICT in the public sector, particularly through e-government initiatives, has become a policy priority for many developing country governments. Notably in tune with the Millennium Development Goal 3, e-Government represents a significant opportunity to create a mechanism of greater gender equality in basic service delivery, in priority areas such as education, health and social protection. Further, it broadens the range of service providers from central, local governments to private sectors and women NGOs, thereby allowing the services to be more women-driven and women-focused. Ultimately, under a positive cycle of strengthened gender equality in basic service delivery and empowerment of women as users of these services, the true potential of e-Government lies in changing the paradigm of participation and representation of women in society. In this sense, mainstreaming gender equality in e-Government proposes an entry point of discussion as to how to include the empowerment of women in the post-2015 development agenda.

With this background, this research examines 11 selected countries in Asia and the Pacific region regarding their current efforts to promote gender equality in e-Government. It is a result of a year-long data collection and deliberation with experts of the national governments, NGOs, international organizations and academia from a broad range of relevant fields including but not limited to gender, ICT, e-Government, and public and social services. In review of the data from countries including Bangladesh, People's Republic of China, Fiji, India, Indonesia, Republic of Korea, Malaysia, Mongolia, the Philippines, Timor-Leste, and Viet Nam, the research looks at how to define the e-Government for gender equality, who to involve in this discussion, how to analyze and assess the progress, and last but not least, what steps and considerations to take for future efforts. Although the generalizability of the findings beyond the studied countries remains as a limitation of this research, its significance lies in being one of the first comparative, analytical attempts to discuss the gender equality and women's empowerment in relation to current e-Government development.

E-Government and Gender Equality

First and foremost, four thematic areas of inquiry that intersect with gender equality and e-Government have emerged from the research, which include:

- ***Women's access to ICT:*** Gender digital divide is compounded by the significant lack of gender-disaggregated ICT statistics at national, regional and international level which hiders the national policy makers to adequately capture the patterns of ICT access and use by women and to develop relevant policy alternatives.

- ***Capacity development for women***: This pillar refers to the capacity of women in becoming active participants of e-Government, which is closely related to the overall level of gender equality, for instance, educational attainment, income, and other socioeconomic standings. Findings of the study confirmed that ICT and e-Government awareness and capacity of gender experts from the government, NGOs and academia should be considered under this objective.

- **Online public service outreach for women**: Objectives under this pillar should go beyond merely providing an access to the existing national e-Government services, but to design and implement targeted online services for women based on adequate assessment of needs.

- **Women's participation in online public process**: This pillar includes gender mainstreaming within the national e-Government framework, with an aim to bring about a more gender-friendly public administration approach. In addition, it is important to consider the potential of women's *online* participation to transform the *offline* reality, using the e-Government as an important vehicle.

Measuring the Readiness

The uptake and adoption of e-Government initiatives can be assured with a multi-faceted assessment surrounding the provision of e-Government infrastructure and services from the government -- the supply side -- as well as sufficient capacity of women – the demand side. This research adapts the methodology of the United Nation e-Government Development Index (EGDI) as the main analysis framework to explore the capacity and progress of e-Government programmes to promote gender equality.

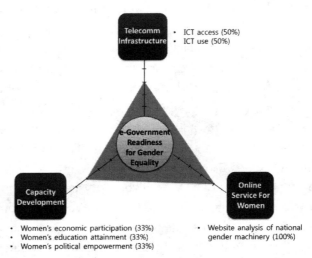

Analyitical Framework of e-Government Readiness for Gender Equality Index

The analytical framework comprises three key pillars including *Telecommunication Infrastructure*, *Capacity Development*, and *Online Service for Women*, which can be tailored for use by countries to assess their level of e-Government readiness and commitment to gender equality through e-Government. According to the level of advancement in each pillar, development phases of e-Government for women can be categorized into the following four conceptual phases.

- **Phase 1: Emerging** This phase entails the usage of ICT to expand access to government information which is of importance to women.
- **Phase 2: Enhanced** The enhanced phase pertains to enhancing the involvement of women and women groups in the process of government activities.
- **Phase 3: Transactional** In this phase, gender programmes that are specially tailored to online delivery are provided, allowing for a complete sense of online transaction.
- **Phase 4: Connected** The connected phase alludes to the stage where government has gone through the full transformation process and all the citizen services are made available online through a single virtual counter 24/7.

Key Findings

- ***Defining the scope of e-Government objectives for gender inclusion:***
  The findings of this study confirm that the scope of gender objectives for e-Government should not only include realizing gender equality in online public service outreach in a gender-neutral sense, but also embrace the potential to use e-Government as a vehicle of women's empowerment in public decision-making process. The objectives could be categorized into four core areas including women's access to ICT, their ICT capacity, public service outreach for women and their participation into society through online channels.

- ***Online service delivery for women***
  The service levels of the researched countries strongly correlate with the country's level of telecommunication infrastructure development compared to other factors considered in this research. The result indicates that surmounting the digital divide is one of the pre-requisites to achieving a greater impact of e-Government for women's empowerment. In addition, an increasing emphasis must be put on the assessment of the level of service usage and user satisfaction, as to how online services are effectively meeting the demands of women, and more fundamentally, to ensure whether the e-Government environment is conducive in creating such a demand from women.

- ***Integration and coordination***
  The result of this study revealed that there is a significant gap between the two realms core to the process of gender mainstreaming in e-Government – women's capacity development and e-Government development. In most of the surveyed countries, respondents stated that gender initiatives have not been fully incorporated in the national ICT and e-Government policies, with risks of isolation and horizontal fragmentation. Many respondents suggested that gender mainstreaming in e-Government should be ultimately led by an apex organization of national ICT and e-Government development, while the national gender machinery has to provide sufficient domain knowledge expertise during the process.

E-Government for Gender Equality Action Plan

The following presents a set of suggested steps to formulate a national action plan to carry out e-Government initiatives for greater gender inclusion.

- ***Understand readiness: country grouping:*** It is important to understand where the policy priority should be placed among the myriads of tasks entailed in the process.

- ***Define a national vision for gender inclusion in e-Government:*** A *vision statement* should define what it means to promote greater gender equality in the e-Government initiative and what aims it should achieve through this measure.

- **Raise awareness:** Priority should be placed on formulating two-tier communication strategy, one targeting the top-level *political leadership* and the other aiming the *broader public*.

- **Establish a focal organization:** It is critical to establish a model of *inter-agency coordination* for gender inclusion and thus identify an entity across the government agencies to serve as focal points for e-Government provision for women.

- **Establish a gender database:** *Gender-disaggregated data collection* of different dimensions of ICT environments is critical to adequately understand the current gender gap and use the findings to create policies for improved relevancy and impact.

- **Build human capacity:** There are two distinct aspects when it comes to capacity building: first, to enhance ICT literacy of women to ensure their equitable access to e-Government initiatives as a traditionally marginalized service recipient; second, to generate and promote the ICT service capacity of government officials and staffs within the national gender machinery as the main provider of e-Government services for women.

- **Ensure technology access for women:** The choice of technologies for e-Government developments should reflect the current level of infrastructure maturity across the country. Among others, two options can be considered: first, ensuring connectivity to existing resources such as public kiosks, libraries and schools; second, selecting and focusing on appropriate technologies for women, most notably by using the mobile platform to provide m-Government initiatives.

- **Define laws and policies pertaining to women's ICT use:** While many of the legal frameworks overlap with general requirements for national e-Government planning, there are several issues that require particular consideration for women, for example, safeguarding public information and privacy against potential ICT-based gender violence.

- **Establish a network of partners:** It is suggested to form a network of partners that comprise organizations and agencies that can effectively assist and participate in the implementation of e-Government for gender inclusion initiatives, including NGOs, research and training institutes, and international / regional organizations.

- **Identify and implement pilot projects:** Selecting the right project to be the 'pilot' is very important, since a successful project becomes a powerful selling point for all future efforts and creates a political momentum to move the initiative ahead. Example areas for a flagship project may include: income generation, education, health, social safety net, and information service for women.

1. Introduction

The adoption of ICT in the public sector, particularly through e-Government initiatives, has become a policy priority for many developing country governments. The increased level of international attention on e-Government promotion combined with national efforts to streamline its public service led to a dramatic expansion of e-Government provision worldwide in recent years. According to the UN e-Government Development Index 2010, 98% of governments have online presence either by having a national portal or ministry websites (UN DESA, 2010). The overall quality of e-Government service has also changed significantly across the globe, driven by the advancement of more inclusive technologies such as Web 2.0, as it moves away from a one-way information provision to a more interactive and participatory forum.

Although the specific objectives of e-Government may vary in each country, e-Government is universal in its aim to increase efficiency and equity of government services, thus supporting sustainable human development. Notably, the potential of e-Government towards achieving the Millennium Development Goals (MDGs) and sustainable development has been well-recognized. In areas where people have limited access to social services and economic opportunities, e-Government may serve as a mechanism of basic service delivery for MDG progress, particularly for the vulnerable population. E-Government also provides a communication channel through which citizens not only gain information on the availability of services, but also ask for greater accountability and transparency in service delivery.

Particularly in tune with MDG 3, e-Government represents a significant opportunity to create a mechanism of greater gender equality in basic service delivery. In priority areas such as education, health and social protection, e-Government facilitates improvements in service availability, and reduces the political, economic and socio-cultural barriers women face in accessing those public resources. Further, it broadens the range of service providers from central, local governments to private sectors and women NGOs, thereby allowing the services to be more women-driven and women-focused. Ultimately, under a positive cycle of strengthened gender equality in basic service delivery and empowerment of women as users of these services, the true potential of e-Government lies in changing the paradigm of participation and representation of women in society. In this sense, mainstreaming gender equality in e-Government proposes an entry point of discussion as to how to include the empowerment of women in the post-2015 development agenda. (Box 1)

However, with myriad obstacles including inequalities in the access to Information and Communication Technology (ICT) and the availability of online contents and services for women, this potential is yet to be realized. Moreover, there is an increasing concern of women's exclusion from such online public services, due largely to the existing socioeconomic inequalities women face in the society such as education and income gaps, as well as under-representation in political and economic decision-making process. Further, since most e-Government applications are recent developments, many developing countries tend to focus on deploying e-Governance strategies at a general level, but not yet on addressing the specific needs of marginalized groups including women. In addition to such an inadequate level of support environment at the national level, international policy support in the e-Government arena exhibits a disparity between the perception and the practice in promoting e-Government that embraces gender equality as an important goal. In sum, the potential of gender equality in *online* service to transform the *offline* reality has not bloomed yet.

With this background, this research examines 11 selected countries in Asia and the Pacific region regarding their current efforts to promote greater gender equality in e-Government. It is a result of a year-long data collection and deliberation with experts of the national governments, NGOs, international organizations and academia from a broad range of relevant fields including but not limited to gender, ICT, e-Government, public and social services.

Box 1

Scoping Gender Equality for the Post-2015 Agenda

At the inaugurating wICT4D conference organized by UN Women and the U.S. Secretary of State's Office held in December 2012, the post-2015 agenda for gender equality was placed at the centerpiece of discussion. Among others, Gurumurthy, Nandini and Saloranta from *IT for Change* have put forth by far one of the most comprehensive policy recommendations to be included in the post-2015 global development agenda. The following summarizes the key content of their report.

The emergent information or network society context offers a range of opportunities for women and girls to enhance their participation across economic, socio-cultural and public-political realms of life, as well as the scope for enhancing their individual freedoms. The Post-2015 agenda therefore, both in terms of goals and related targets and indicators, has to promote and measure women's participation in the information society and their access to and effective use of the Internet and ICTs.

1. *There should be a specific goal related to the meaningful and effective use of ICTs and the Internet which is measured through gender sensitive targets and indicators. This should take into account the quality of access, and not just availability.*
2. *There should be a specific goal related to gender equality and women's and girls' empowerment that takes into account access to and effective use of ICTs and the Internet as a target (with appropriate indicators) within the goal. The larger goal of women's empowerment in the contemporary information society cannot be dis-embedded from the context that ICTs are creating.*
3. *To facilitate a nuanced assessment, the indicators that are evolved under the above-mentioned goals must capture the individual-household, public-institutional and community-social aspects of access to, and use of, ICTs and the Internet.*

Source: *Through the 'information society' prism: Scoping gender equality for the post-2015 agenda*, Anita Gurumurthy, Nandini.C and Emma Saloranta, wICT4D conference Position Paper, IT for Change, January 2013
http://www.itforchange.net/sites/default/files/ITfC/Through%20the%20information%20society%20prism%20-%20Scoping%20gender%20equality%20for%20the%20post-2015%20agenda.pdf

Accessed on February 10, 2013.

By employing a combination of methods including web service analysis, online policy survey and in-depth interviews of experts from the 11 countries, the research draws out policy implications aimed for broader audiences in the region, who share the interest to improve gender equality in the online public services at the national, regional and local level. The discussion includes how to define the e-Government for gender equality, who to involve in this discussion and how to organize the collective, how to analyze and assess the progress, and last but not least, what steps and considerations to take for future efforts.

However, it should be mentioned at the beginning that the study, due to the small number of countries reviewed and the limitation in data collection, does not provide a generalizable prescription to decision-makers. Nevertheless, the research has its significance in initializing a comparable analysis of online-based public services for women in the region, from advanced countries to emerging countries, and in forming a linkage among different areas of gender equality, public service and ICT development. In this sense, the findings drawn from this attempt bear a certain degree of relevance applicable to countries in different stages of e-Government development and gender equality, and offer a reference point against which policy makers can evaluate the country progress by themselves.

The first chapter will present a conceptual overview of e-Government and its implication to greater gender equality in public administration and sustainable national development. The following chapter will suggest an analysis framework to assess the readiness of a country's gender initiative in e-Government, based on the result of 11 country examples that were selected according to key country characteristics shared in Asia and the Pacific region. Finally, a toolkit to set up a national action plan for gender equality in e-Government will be presented, which includes components such as the readiness assessment, web development and gender database.

1.1   E-Government and Gender Equality

In general, e-government is defined as "the use by government agencies of information technologies such as Wide Area Networks, the Internet, and mobile computing that have the ability to transform relations with citizens, businesses, and other arms of government" (World Bank, 2009). The objectives of e-Government vary in each country; however, in all cases, should transcend the mere efficiency of governmental processes and move towards devising methods that allow social, political and economic changes, thereby enhancing sustainable and equitable human development.

Adopting this notion of e-Government, an important question arises as to how to define the scope of objectives to improve gender equality in e-Government. Inherently, e-Government is gender-neutral in a sense that it provides online access of core public services to citizens in general. In this case, would it suffice to focus on improving women's access to ICT so that women would eventually have equal opportunity to use e-Government services? Or should the gender objectives go beyond the provision of equal access to e-Government, and consider including the potential to change the concepts of participation and representativeness of women in the public decision making process, and ultimately, to transform the relationship between women and the government, and the society as a whole?

Interestingly, the findings of this study confirm that the scope of gender objectives for e-Government should not only include realizing gender equality in online public service outreach, but also embrace the potential to use e-Government as a vehicle of women's empowerment in public decision-making process.[1] In this regard, the discussion to define the scope of objectives should consider the following four keywords, ICT, women, e-Government, and participation. Accordingly, the four pillars of gender equality in e-Government emerged from the research, which include: women's access to ICT, capacity development for women, online public service outreach for women, and women's participation in online public process. It should be the specific situation of a country's advancement and capacity in those four pillars that jointly influence the scope and priority of objectives for gender equality in e-Government.

---

[1] For the brevity of discussion throughout this report, 'gender equality in e-Government' will be used as an umbrella term to embrace the scope of gender concerns identified from the findings, which include gender equality in e-Government as well as empowerment of women through e-Government. It should be noted that the two concepts, gender equality and empowerment of women, are different in their meanings – gender equality emphasizes remedying the existing inequality between men and women which reproduces further inequalities with negative consequences for women's well-being; while empowerment of women does not have a connotation of gender disparities and focuses on the changes needed for women to realize her full human rights (UNFPA, 2012). Since women's empowerment is usually considered as a way to achieve gender equality, the two terms accompany each other in most development literature regarding women, notably MDG3. MDG3 reflects the strong belief by the development community that redressing gender inequality and empowering women is an important development objective on grounds of both fairness and efficiency.

The following table shows the linkages between four objectives of e-Government for gender equality and the respective dimensions of the analysis framework used in this research.

[Table 1] Objectives of e-Government for Gender Equality

Dimensions of Analytical Framework	Objectives of e-Government For Gender Equality
Women's access to ICT	Improving women's e-Government access • Affordability of service • Location/ number of facility
Capacity development for women	Improving women's capacity to use e-Government • Information literacy • Availability of assistance, training opportunities
Online service for women	Improving e-Government service for women • Availability of service • Quality and relevancy
Online participation of women	Improving women's participation in/through e-Government • Gender advocacy and networking • Monitoring

Access to ICT

One of the critical prerequisites for e-Government to support gender equality is women's **access to ICT**. A great number of existing researches have addressed the issue of gender digital divide. However, the findings of this study revealed that it is compounded by the significant lack of gender-disaggregated ICT statistics at national, regional and international level which hiders the national policy makers to adequately capture the patterns of ICT access and use by women and to develop relevant policy alternatives. In this regard, the gender objectives of e-Government should address the collection and analysis of baseline data on the ground.

Capacity development

The second issue refers to the **capacity** of women in becoming active participants of e-Government, which is closely related to the overall level of gender equality, for instance, in educational attainment, income, and other socioeconomic standings. Particularly, the use of e-Government requires the user to attain a certain level of ICT capacity, which encompasses a set of computer and technical skills, as well as basic literacy and numeracy. In addition to the capacity of women as an individual from the demand side of e-Government, it is also critical to strengthen the supply side capacity. Findings of the study confirm that ICT and e-Government awareness and capacity of gender experts from the government, NGOs and academia should be considered under this objective.

Online Service Outreach

The **relevancy of contents and services** often serves as a strong incentive for users to adopt new technology (Avgerou, 2010; Alampay & Umali, 2007). In this sense, it is critical to ensure that contents and information which adequately reflect women's needs are available through e-Government in an adequate format. However, in policy practice, the importance of contents relevancy as an incentive to boost up women's demands on e-Government is often neglected within the national-level e-Government vision. The findings of this research reveal that online public service for women should go beyond merely providing an access to the existing national e-Government services, and design and implement targeted online services for women based on adequate assessment of needs.

Participation

Coupled with relevant political support, e-Government can go a long way in facilitating greater gender equality within the benefits of public service and support, and in making a positive influence to address the deep-rooted socioeconomic inequalities women face as a whole. Findings of this research confirm that the gender objectives should include **gender mainstreaming** within the national e-Government framework, with an aim to bring about a more gender-friendly public administration approach. In addition, it is important to consider the potential of women's *online* participation to transform the *offline* reality, using the e-Government as an important vehicle.

Overall, securing a channel of **participation for women** through e-government innovation symbolizes a significant opportunity. The crucial elements of the application of ICT for gender equality in governance in this regard is to reinvent the public sector by transforming its internal and external way of handling activities, as well as its interrelationships with women and other actors in the society.

Major benefits of e-Government for gender equality are discussed below.

- Improving efficiency in the design and delivery of government services for women
- Improving equitable access to and delivery of public services and information targeted for women
- Enhancing the openness and transparency of gender administration and engagement with women
- Increasing the capacity of women to be active participants of the information society
- Contributing to achieving the MDG and sustainable development of a country with economic and social outcomes

1.2   Forms of Interactions in e-Government: Gender Implications

Although the entire gamut of e-Government involves a large number of entities and processes, there are primarily four types of interaction which form the foundation of e-government application for greater gender equality.

[Table 2] E-Government: Stakeholders and Domains

Types	Goals
G2C (Citizens)	To provide easier **access** to government information, improved delivery of services and welfare benefits To reinforce **participation in the local community** and networks
G2B (Business)	To allow transaction initiatives i.e. e-procurement and e-commerce for **reduction of cost and red tape**
G2G (Government)	To **integrate** national, regional and local governments for a seamless **single point access** for citizens
G2E (Employees)	To provide **learning and knowledge sharing** among government employees

Source: Heeks, 2001

G2G (Government to Government)

The interaction involves sharing data and the conduct of information exchange among various government departments and other entities via electronic means. The exchange could be both intra- and inter-agency at the national level, as well as across national, provincial and local levels. In the context of G2G interactions targeted toward improving gender equality, activities may include the establishment of gender statistics and relevant data sources that integrate national, regional, and local governments through a seamless single point access. By automating and integrating many of the gender-related administrative tasks and data transaction across different levels of government agencies, it has a potential to bring about a more coordinated policy development as well as an effective monitoring of gender impact.

G2C (Government to Citizen/Women)

This category includes interactions where electronic dissemination of information as well as electronic delivery of services takes place, fulfilling the primary objective of e-Government. Initiatives in this form of interaction attempt to make traditional on-spot based transactions less time-consuming and more convenient. Moreover, they open an avenue of women's participation in the process and formulation of government policies. With this aspect, e-Government allows women a greater access to public service and welfare benefits in terms of the scope, variety, and to a different degree, the ease of use and quality, i.e. obtaining certificates or registering and applying to government programmes for women. In addition, it provides an open space for policy input by offering an easy entry point of participation for local women's communities, networks, and NGOs, and facilitates interactions beyond sectoral boundaries among public agencies, businesses and civil society.

G2B (Government to Business)

The interaction aims to improve efficiency of the procurement of goods and services by the government from the commercial business entities. The more sophisticated forms of this interaction take place in the transaction and exchange between the government and businesses regarding the licenses, taxation and policies issued for various sectors. It has a potential for creating new and innovative products and services for women and invigorating business sectors related to women's livelihood, as the improved practice of procurement may lead to cost reduction and increased efficiency. Women entrepreneurs may also benefit from e-procurement and e-commerce practices that allow access to targeted information on government policies and procurement opportunities.

G2E (Government to Employee)

The interaction in this category promotes learning and knowledge sharing among government employees. In particular, G2E interaction can contribute to the improvement of institutional capacity in gender policy development and delivery within the existing national machinery of gender equality, through online based training programmes and work guidelines, rules and regulations. It can also contribute to identifying and recruiting external specialists for specific government programmes with targeted employment opportunities for gender specialists, and building a base for a community of practice (CoP) that covers individuals and institutions within and beyond the government agencies.

1.3   Development Phases of e-Government for Women

E-Government application generally goes through various stages such as publishing of information on the website to carrying out transactions. The UN e-Government Development Index (EGDI) has formulated a four-stage e-Government model which can serve as a reference for government to position where a project fits in the overall evolution of a national e-Government strategy (UN DESA, 2012)[2].

Initiatives to improve gender equality in e-Government should also consider different phases of application and development. The maturity stages of e-Government for Gender Equality, which is an adaptation of the EGDI's four-stage model, suggest key characteristics of the e-Government evolution regarding the usefulness of contents and services, technical sophistication and ease of use, degree of integration, etc. While the assessment of online service in EGDI is conducted by examining a country's overall, comprehensive quality of services from the national e-Government

---

[2] See Box   for further information on the four-stage categorization of UN e-Government Development. The framework was used for the analysis of national gender machinery websites from 11 countries presented in Chapter 3 of this report.

portal and websites of key ministries including but not limited to education, health, finance, and labor, the adapted gender model considers specific online services targeted for women, notably through the website of national gender machinery.[3]

However, it is worth mentioning that since the model is a conceptual framework, the maturity phases are neither linear nor categorical, and it does not imply that all governments have to go through all of these phases.

[Figure 1] E-Government and Gender Equality: Development Phases

Stage 1 Emerging	Stage 2 Enhanced	Stage 3 Transactional	Stage 4 Connected
Information Dissemination	Access	Service Delivery Capacity	Citizen Participation
Outreach	Usability		Interconnectedness
Online Presence	Stakeholder Intake	Online Transactions	Integration & Transformation

Targeted e-Government Initiatives For Gender Equality

• Creation of website(s) for the national gender machinery • Organization structure and contact information • Static content links for gender policies and programmes • Links to websites of related agencies and networks	• More sophisticated websites with interaction capacity • Email newsletter subscription and SNS links of national gender machinery • Downloadable forms and data for specific gender polices and programmes	• Provision of complete online-based gender programmes • Secure identity authentication and individualized services • Available services including online registration and application to gender programmes and issuance of certificates, e-learning, etc.	• Integration with national government portal • One-stop public service window across government agencies, with services clustered among common needs • Transformation of gender governance through integration of information, services and participation

Source: UN DESA, 2012

---

[3] Further explanation on the assessment methodology will be given in Chapter 2.

Box 2

Four-Stage Model of e-Government – Online Service
UN e-Government Development Index (EGDI) 2012

Stage I - Emerging:
Government websites provide information on public policy, governance, laws, regulations, relevant documentation and government services provided. They have links to ministries, departments and other branches of government. Citizens are easily able to obtain information on what is new in the national government and ministries and have links to archived information.

Stage II - Enhanced:
Government websites deliver enhanced one-way or simple two-way e-communication between government and citizen, such as downloadable forms for government services and applications. The sites have audio and video capabilities and are multi-lingual. This also includes some limited e-services where citizens can request non-electronic forms and request for personal information, which will be mailed to their house.

Stage III - Transactional:
Government websites engage in two-way communication with their citizens, including requesting and receiving inputs on government policies, programmes, regulations, etc. In this stage, transactions require some form of electronic authentication of the citizen's identity to successfully complete the exchange.

Stage IV - Connected:
Government websites have changed the way to communicate with their citizens, and they are proactive in requesting information and opinions from the citizens using web 2.0 and other interactive tools. The e-services and e-solutions that are available cut across the departments and ministries in a seamless manner. Information, data and knowledge is transferred from government agencies through integrated applications.

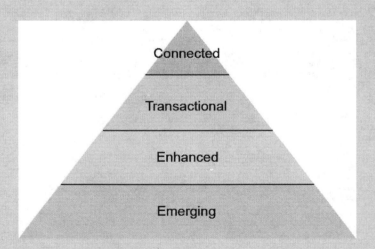

Excerpted from UN e-Government Survey Homepage at
http://www2.unpan.org/egovkb/egovernment_resources/Spotlights_2010.html

Phase 1: Emerging

This phase entails the usage of ICT to expand access to government information which is of importance to women. An efficient use of ICT can disseminate government information to a broader audience in a fast and convenient manner. At the initial stage of national e-Government development, an ideal point of entry for developing countries would be setting up a website for the national gender machinery. The website, as an official gateway to gender-related policies and programmes, would provide a ready access to online information ranging from the organizational structure of the national gender machinery to government statistics, publications, government services and programmes aimed for women's empowerment.

An example of this emerging level is Timor-Leste, where the national gender machinery, the Secretary of State for the Promotion of Equality (SSPE) has recently launched its website with an aim to better reach out to its constituents via online means.

Example(s) of this level:
- Bangladesh, Ministry of Women and Child Affairs (http://www.mowca.gov.bd)
- Fiji, Ministry of Women, Culture and Social Welfare (http://www.women.fiji.gov.fj/)
- Timor-Leste, Secretary of State for the Promotion of Equality (http://sepi.gov.tl)

Phase 2: Enhanced

The enhanced phase pertains to enhancing the involvement of women and women groups in the process of government activities. Through the use of technology, the interaction between the governments and women can be stimulated and become more effective. Basic forms of interactivity available through emails, downloadable forms, discussion forums and online polls not only provide an improved delivery of basic services, but also build up a basis for online participation.

An example of this level is Indonesia, where the Ministry website provides key features for usability and access, and delivers basic online service via downloadable forms for its programmes and features such as online library.

Example(s) of this level:
- People's Republic of China, National Working Committee on Women and Children (http://www.nwccw.gov.cn/)
- Indonesia, Ministry of Women Empowerment and Child Protection (http://www.menegpp.go.id/)
- The Philippines, Philippine Commission on Women (http://pcw.gov.ph/)

Phase 3: Transactional

In this phase, gender programmes that are specially tailored to online delivery are provided, allowing for a complete sense of online transaction. Services demonstrate the advancement of technology and programme expertise such as digital certificates, applications and other personalized services, and service users can carry out the transaction without having to visit the government office. Through web kiosks and other applications, the government can pursue a targeted approach for specific population via internet, allowing for greater service effectiveness, relevance and outreach for the women population in society.

An example of this transactional level is Malaysia, where the Ministry provides a number of targeted online services including e-learning and online petition. A basic level of personalized services is available notably through its financial management system for single parents.

Example(s) of this level:
- India, Ministry of Women and Child Development (http://wcd.nic.in/)
- Malaysia, Ministry of Women, Family and Community Development (http://www.kpwkm.gov.my/)

Phase 4: Connected

The connected phase alludes to the stage where government has gone through the full transformation process and citizen services are made available online through a single virtual counter 24/7. Through these integrated services, national policies and programmes can achieve a greater coherence to the gender empowerment principle, with an increased potential to streamline the gender impact of such policies. In addition, improved coordination and monitoring may lead to greater organizational changes across the government and further in the society, aligning organizational setup with new capacities and integrating the operations and infrastructure.

An example of this connected level is Republic of Korea, where the national gender machinery website provides a variety of targeted, secure, and personalized online services for women including real-time online counseling, e-learning and talent registration system. The website is interconnected with the national e-Government portal which includes key participatory features such as online petition, citizen proposal and information disclosure request.

Example(s) of this level:
- Republic of Korea, Ministry of Gender Equality and Family (http://www.mogef.go.kr)

1.4   Stakeholders

The adoption of e-Government in any country involves active participation and the contribution of a number of key players and stakeholders in the entire process. In the application of e-Government initiatives for women, such a multi-stakeholder approach is essential to coordinate the communication gap between gender and ICT ministries alongside their respective policies.

[Figure 2] Gender Equality and e-Government: Stakeholders

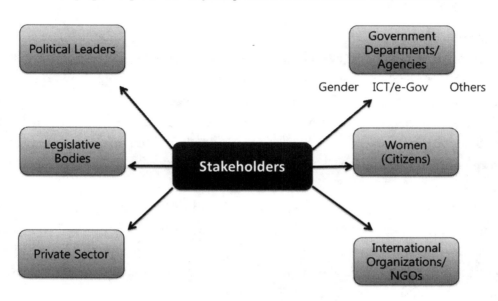

Political leaders
It is essential to have a strong political leadership of the country to be fully sensitized towards the gender imperative of the national e-Government strategy, and to provide relevant political support for realization of such a vision.

Its crucial role is displayed in all levels of e-Government development for women. On one hand, in emerging level countries, the role of political leadership is critical to make a head start. For example in Timor-Leste, the inaugural appointment of Secretary of State for the Promotion of Equality in 2006 eventually led to the decision to develop a website of national gender administration for the first time. On the other hand, at a more advanced level of development, for example in Republic of Korea, the national gender informatization policy was promoted under the strong political support during the early 2000, which played a pivotal role in moving the country towards connected level of e-Government development for women.

Government departments/ agencies
Government departments at all levels need to ensure a synchronized back-end integration of systems and processes in order to achieve a smooth and seamless transformation of e-Government systems. Particularly at the early stages of e-Government development, the coordination and

balance between the gender programme expertise and ICT / e-Government technology capacity are essential. The level of awareness, willingness to change, technical capacity among government employees and the collective institutional energy also play a key role.

The inter-agency coordination becomes particularly important when a country reaches at the late-enhanced level of development. In order to achieve seamless transactions in and out of its online services, for example as seen in the case of Malaysia and Republic of Korea, tasks such as back-end integration of systems and connection with the national e-Government portal should be achieved.

Gender departments/ agencies

As the representative agency specialized in the gender policies and programmes, it is essential that national gender department/ agencies have the institutional and human capacity to translate their programme knowledge into actual functions of online services, conceptually and to a certain degree, technically. Even though its key role should be maintained through all stages of the maturity model, the internal capacity becomes critical when a country is moving from an emerging to an enhanced level.

For example, Malaysia and Republic of Korea have a competent, functioning ICT division within their national gender machineries, while countries such as Fiji, Timor-Leste are currently delegating the task of online service delivery to third parties. By nurturing in-house ICT experts and keeping track of the organizational memory concerning online public service for women, a country can make a smooth, successful transition to the next level.

ICT departments/ agencies

As a country gradually makes advancement towards a more integrated national e-Government portal, it becomes more important to have a close tie and coordination between the gender department and the ICT/ e-Government department. As the ICT department plays a key role in the provision of infrastructure and integration of services and systems, gender policies should be well-integrated with national ICT and e-Government plans throughout their implementation and monitoring processes. Conversely, ICT department may play a proactive role to include women as one of its priority beneficiary groups. For instance in India, Department of Electronics and Information Technology (DEIT) has conducted women digital literacy scheme as part of its National e-Government Plan, with an aim to expand its service coverage to disadvantaged rural women.

Legislative bodies

The formulation and enactment of well-crafted laws and policies are pre-requisite to the success of e-Government for greater gender equality, as it is directly related to the resource allocation and designation of responsible agencies.

It should play a key role whenever a country is trying to make a leap in between stages; as noted, the cases of Republic of Korea's National Gender Informatization policy (2001-2006) and People's

Republic of China's National Programme for Women's Development (2011-2020) are illustrative examples under which the development of national policies set out necessary financial and institutional arrangement for the next step.

Women (Citizens)

Being the key beneficiaries of the entire process, their role is crucial in defining the service needs and demands, as well as identifying fast and convenient delivery methods of online-based information and programmes. They can also contribute effectively to the process of policy making by voicing their opinions and views electronically. Particularly, the ultimate contribution of gender equality in e-Government should lie in paving a way for women to participate in the society through online means. In this sense, the role of women in the process should evolve from an object to a subject – from a passive receiver of services at an early stage of development to a proactive provider of input at a more advanced stage.

Interactive online petition systems found in the cases of India and Republic of Korea may serve as a vehicle to strengthen the role of women in this regard. Also, the increasing use of social network services (SNS) in public outreach for feedback as observed in the Philippines can be considered a new avenue of women's participation.

Private sector

A synergetic collaboration and partnership across the government, ICT industry, and private sector entities lead to an easier fulfillment of e-Government goals for a greater gender equality. Particularly, the private sector plays a key role in not only potentially bringing in new technologies, expertise and service models, but also increasing e-Government access for women, i.e. through targeted internet / mobile internet subscription plans for women and other services designed for women's information needs and use behavior. The engagement of private sector in gender-related online service is observed in countries at enhanced stages such as India, Indonesia and the Philippines, where auction and bidding information are available under separate G2B section of the gender machinery website.

NGOs and international organizations

NGOs and international organizations can play an important role by serving as facilitators and motivators of the national e-Government initiatives for women. As mentioned, the gender imperative in e-Government is a subject which receives an ever-growing attention in the international development arena. Through effective promotion of its value, these agencies can raise awareness of common citizens, national government agencies, and the international community. In addition, they can contribute to research in the area, exchanges of good practices among countries, and promotion of cooperative activities at regional and international levels. At the initial stage, a partnership with international organizations may provide an impetus for greater financial support and knowledge transfer.

For example, the Info Lady programme in Bangladesh, which aims to extend the online service outreach for rural women, was conducted as a collaboration project of the UNDP country office in Bangladesh.[4] At a domestic level engagement with NGOs, India has an online community of existing women NGOs called e-AWEDAN, which aims to strengthen the online presence and capacity of NGOs to broaden the service base.[5]

---

[4] See Box   in the section 3.1.1.Bangladesh for more information on this initiative.
[5] See Box in the section 3.2.3.Integration and Coordination for more information on this programme.

2. Measuring Readiness

2.1   The Concept

With the specter of the growing digital exclusion, the political, economic, social and cultural aspects related to women's ICT access and capacity assumes a paramount position in the roadmap towards e-Government. The uptake and adoption of e-Government initiatives can be assured with a multi-faceted assessment; on one hand, the provision of e-Government infrastructure and services from the government from the supply side, as well as sufficient capacity of women from the demand side, on the other. Hence, before a country embarks on a journey towards an application of e-Government for greater gender equality, it will be useful to assess the state of readiness in a number of different aspects, notably, the levels of ICT development, women's capacity development, and e-Government development.

Though the generalizability of such a readiness framework is difficult to achieve, an analytical attempt to develop a comparable assessment model for gender equality in e-Government carries certain significance. First, it fills the gap in the existing international policy discussions of gender, public administration and ICT. By examining the broad scope of issues these three key areas concern and by drawing out core common areas where the imperatives and interests meet, the framework provides a set of focused pointers to policy makers. Also, the framework presents a systematic method to diagnose a country's preparedness that is to a certain degree internationally comparable. Policy makers can understand where it stands according to the important pillars of gender equality for e-Government and find priority areas where it needs more strategic efforts. Lastly, the international comparison of strengths and weaknesses in readiness allows room for cooperation and knowledge sharing among countries at international, regional and bilateral levels.

The following section provides an illustrative model that displays different aspects to consider when developing e-Government efforts to support gender equality. It also presents an analytical framework which can be tailored for use by other countries to assess their level of e-Government readiness and commitment to gender equality through e-Government.

2.2   Analytical Framework

This research adapts the methodology of the United Nation e-Government Development Index (EGDI) as the main analysis framework to explore the capacity and progress of e-Government programmes to promote gender equality (UN DESA, 2012). As e-Government efforts to improve gender equality are relatively new in many developing countries in Asia and the Pacific region, adopting and culturally contextualizing an established framework may increase its usefulness and adoption. However, the choice of whether to adopt an approach or model that is already considered to be a standard benchmark or to formulate an assessment methodology that is either new or customized lies solely with the country aiming to conduct the assessment. This decision depends on the conditions particular to that country and the time and resources that are available.

For the purpose of this report, the methodology used in the EGDI is revised to reflect gender concerns in e-Government development. The revised *Analysis Framework for Gender equality in e-Government* is shown in the following table, which aims to help identify a country's readiness and progress to integrate gender equality in e-Government strategies. We have renamed the three dimensions from the EGDI, Online Service Index, Telecommunication Index, and Human Capital Index respectively into *Telecommunication Infrastructure, Capacity Development,* and *Online Service for Women.*

In addition to the three main dimensions of EGDI, the fourth dimension, *Online Participation* was also considered. As the EGDI states, promoting participation of the citizen, in this report with the particular emphasis on women, is the cornerstone of socially inclusive governance. Indeed, in a sense that the participation dimension is directly related to both demand and supply side of e-Government and the overall impact of e-Government, its importance should not be underestimated.

However, due to the difficulties of collecting the opinions of the citizens towards e-Government as a participatory tool, currently, the e-Participation index of EGDI is measured in a limited capacity and is only provided as a supplementary index to the main EGDI.[6] For this research, difficulties of a similar nature arose: the limited logistical capacity to measure opinions of women e-Government users from 11 countries. Furthermore, the purpose of this analysis framework lies in measuring the country readiness to facilitate gender equality initiative in e-Government rather than assessing its outcome. Therefore, while notwithstanding the importance of women's online participation as one of the key objectives of e-Government for gender equality, it was decided to exclude the online participation from the main analysis framework at this time.

Telecommunication Infrastructure

This dimension mainly concerns the general physical connectivity of e-Government services. Even though it would be ideal to utilize gender-disaggregated data for the purpose of this study, the lack of such comparable data availability significantly limits this possibility.

Due to this limitation, the infrastructure dimension data adopts the non-gender-disaggregated statistics on ICT access and use from the latest ICT Development Index (IDI) 2011 from the International Telecommunication Union (ITU) as shown in the table below.

---

[6] For the 2012 survey, the e-Participation index was assessed only for the G2C aspects. For more information on the e-Participation index of the EGDI, see 2012 Survey Homepage at
http://www2.unpan.org/egovkb/egovernment_overview/eparticipation.htm

[Table 3] Measurement of Telecommunication Infrastructure Dimension

Dimension	Variables	Measurement	Sources
Telecommunication Infrastructure	ICT Access	• Fixed-telephone lines per 100 inhabitants • Mobile subscriptions per 100 inhabitants • International Internet bandwidth (bit/s) • Percentage households with a computer • Percentage households with Internet	IDI, 2011
	ICT Use	• Percentage individuals using Internet • Broadband Internet subscriptions per 100 • Mobile-broadband subscriptions per 100	IDI, 2011

Source: ITU 2011

Capacity Development

This dimension measures gender equality in each country as a proxy to assess women's relative capacity to use e-Government services. For the measurement of this dimension, two most frequently referenced international indices have been reviewed, including the Global Gender Gap Index (GGGI) published by the World Economic Forum (WEF), and the Gender Inequality Index (GII) published by the United Nations Development Programme (UNDP). The key difference between GGGI and GII lies in the degree to which a country's level of overall development affects the index scores. While GII, developed in part of the UNDP Human Development Index (HDI) reflects a country's level of socioeconomic development such as income and educational attainment, GGGI focuses on measuring the gender-based gaps in access to resources and opportunities in individual countries rather than the actual levels of the available resources and opportunities in those countries.

Noting this conceptual difference, data for *Capacity Development* dimension was derived from the 2011 GGGI for the following reasons. First, the purpose of this analysis framework lies in identifying the comparative strengths and weaknesses of each three dimensions within an individual country rather than providing an international ranking of countries. In this sense, an index which is more independent from countries' the levels of development and is more focused on the actual gender gap would better serve the purpose of this exercise and assist in formulating country-specific policy prescriptions. Second, the other two dimensions of the index, *Telecommunication Infrastructure* and *Online Service for Women*, tend to be highly correlated with a country's general level of development as they inherently require certain level of investment. Therefore, the use of GGGI would minimize the duplicative effect of a country's national development in the overall measurement of the index values.

The table below shows the specific composition of indices used to measure the gender development dimension, including: 1) women's economic participation, 2) women's education attainment, and 3) women's political empowerment.

[Table 4] Measurement of Capacity Development Dimension

Dimension	Variables	Measurement	Sources
Capacity Development	Economic Participation	• Ratio: Female labour force participation over male value • Wage equality between women and men for similar work (converted to female-over-male ratio) • Ratio: Estimated female earned income over male value • Ratio: Female legislators, senior officials, managers over male value • Ratio: Female professional/technical workers over male value	GGGI 2011
	Education Attainment	• Ratio: Female literacy rate over male value • Ratio: Female net primary level enrolment over male value • Ratio: Female net secondary level enrolment over male value • Ratio: Female gross tertiary level enrolment over male value	GGGI 2011
	Political Empowerment	• Ratio: Women with seats in parliament over male value • Ratio: Women at ministerial level over male value • Ratio: Number of years of a female head of state or government (last 50 years) over male value	GGGI 2011

Source: WEF 2011

Online Service for Women

This dimension measures the scope and quality of existing online services for women that are provided through the national website of gender machinery or equivalent. As will be further explained in the section 2.4.Data Collection Methodologies, this dimension has been further operationalized to discuss the extent to which ICT supports national gender equality agendas. This is determined by looking at the relevant information and products/services that the national government provides to women.[7] Adopted from the UN e-Government Development Index[8], this

---

[7] Regarding the importance of ICT to support national machineries for gender equality, refer to *"ICT and Gender Equality: New opportunities and challenges for public administration to implement internationally agreed development goals including MDGs"* (United Nations, 2010). Even though the official titles of such machinery differ from country to country, this report will use "Ministry of Gender" as a general term indicating the central machinery of gender equality in a country.

[8] UNDESA's UN e-Government Survey Web Measure Index presents data collected from the assessment of online government services offered through the websites of the Ministries/Departments of Health, Education, Social Welfare, Labor and Finance.

dimension has been measured by analyzing the web content of national governments' gender equity offices and programmes. The analysis examines the type and scope of e-Government services for women, the effectiveness of the provision of content and services reflecting women's needs and interests, and the provision of opportunities for women to participate in policy making process.

[Figure 3] Analysis Framework and Data Source Enrolment

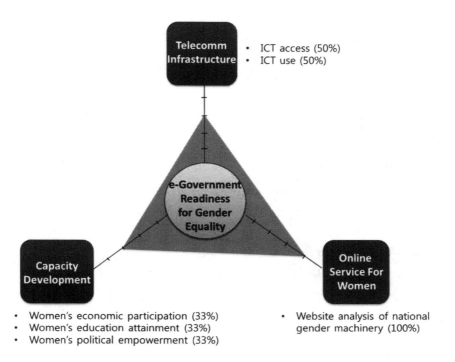

Dimensions	Factors	Source	Measurements	Weight
Telecom Infrastructure	ICT Access	ITU: IDI	1. Fixed-telephone lines per 100 inhabitants 2. Mobile-cellular telephone subscriptions per 100 inhabitants 3. International Internet bandwidth (bit/s) per Internet user 4. Percentage of households with a computer 5. Percentage of households with Internet access	50%
	ICT Use	ITU: IDI	1. Percentage of individuals using the Internet 2. Fixed (wired)-broadband Internet subscriptions per 100 inhabitants 3. Active mobile-broadband subscriptions per 100 inhabitants	50%
Capacity Development	Women's Economic Participation	WEF: GGGI	1. Ratio: Female labour force participation over male value, 2. Wage equality between women and men for similar work (converted to female-over-male ratio) 3. Ratio: Estimated female earned income over male value 4. Ratio: Female legislators, senior officials, managers over male value 5. Ratio: Female professional/technical workers over male value	33%
	Women's Education attainment	WEF: GGGI	1. Ratio: Female literacy rate over male value 2. Ratio: Female net primary level enrolment over male value 3. Ratio: Female net secondary level enrolment over male value 4. Ratio: Female gross tertiary level enrolment over male value	33%
	Women's Political empowerment	WEF: GGGI	1. Ratio: Women with seats in parliament over male value 2. Ratio: Women at ministerial level over male value 3. Ratio: Number of years of a female head of state or government (last 50 years) over male value	33%
Online Service for Women	e-Gov for Women Functionality	National Gender Machinery Web Measurement	1. Information dissemination and outreach 2. Access and usability 3. Service delivery capability 4. Citizen participation and interconnectedness	100%

2.3   Selection of Countries

Countries were selected on the basis of fair representation of the following five criteria, which are most commonly used for sub-grouping countries in Asia and the Pacific region and are supported by internationally available classification methodology.

- Geographical subgroups in Asia and Pacific region (World Bank, 2011)
    1) East Asia and Pacific, and 2) South Asia
- Grouping by income level (World Bank, 2011)
    1) Low income group ($1,025 or less),
    2) Lower-middle income group ($1,026 to $4,035),
    3) Upper-middle income group ($4,036 to $12,475), and
    4) High income group ($12,476 or more)
- Grouping by Human Development (UNDP, 2011)
    1) low, 2) medium, 3) high, and 4) very high
- Grouping by population size (World Bank, 2011)
    1) over 1 billion,
    2) over 100 million to less than 1 billion,
    3) over 10 million to less than 100 million, and
    4) less than 10 million
- Other selected groupings (UN Statistics Division, 2011)[9]
    1) least developed countries,
    2) landlocked developing countries, and
    3) small island developing countries

However, it should be noted that due to the exploratory nature of this study, the selection of countries was conducted in such a way that would at least ensure individual characteristics of a total of 32 countries in Asia and the Pacific region to be fairly represented in the final selection of 11 countries.[10] Consequently, the final selection was conducted considering a combination of multiple categories commonly practiced in international level analyses, rather than through a randomized sampling according to a single selection methodology. Therefore, such methodological restriction may limit the generalizability of the result.

---

[9] In contrast to the other four criteria applied, the categorization under this grouping, by definition, is neither mutually exclusive nor exhaustive.

[10] In its exploratory nature, the research was conducted in two separate phases between which an Expert Group Meeting (EGM) took place to fine-tune the direction of research, country selection criteria, and format of the final outcome. The first phase of research was conducted during July –December 2011 for six countries including Bangladesh, Indonesia, Republic of Korea, Malaysia, the Philippines and Viet Nam. The EGM was conducted in February 2012 in participation of UN agency partners in the region, experts in government, academia and NGOs. The meeting, among other discussions, drew out recommendations on additional countries to be included in the second-phase of the research for a fair representation of the region. The second phase of research took place during August –November 2012 for five additional countries as decided in the EGM including People's Republic of China (country size), Fiji (small island developing country), India (country size), Mongolia (landlocked developing country), and Timor-Leste (least developed country).

A total of 11 countries were selected out of 32 countries in the region, by applying this selection criteria and taking into account the data availability at the time of research. The 11 countries are: Bangladesh, People's Republic of China, Fiji, India, Indonesia, Republic of Korea, Malaysia, Mongolia, the Philippines, Timor-Leste, and Viet Nam. The following figure outlines the categorization of 11 countries according to the selection criteria.

[Figure 4] Selection Criteria and Categorization of Sampled Countries

Geographical Sub-grouping of Asia and the Pacific (WB)	Other Selected Groupings (UN Statistics Division)*	Income Group (WB, 2011)	Human Development Index (UNDP, 2011)	Population Size (WB, 2011)
East Asia and Pacific - People's Republic of China - Fiji - Indonesia - Republic of Korea - Malaysia - Mongolia - Philippines - Timor-Leste - Viet Nam (9 out of 24)	**Least Developed** - Bangladesh - Timor-Leste (2) **Landlocked Developing** - Mongolia (1)	**Low** - Bangladesh (1) **Lower-middle** - Fiji - India - Indonesia - Mongolia - Philippines - Timor-Leste - Viet Nam (7)	**Low** - Bangladesh - Timor-Leste (2) **Medium** - People's Republic of China - Fiji - India - Indonesia - Mongolia - Philippines - Viet Nam (7)	**Over 1 billion** - People's Republic of China - India (2) **100million – 1 billion** - Bangladesh - Indonesia (2) **10 – 100 million** - Republic of Korea - Malaysia - Philippines - Viet Nam (4)
South Asia - Bangladesh - India (2 out of 8)	**Small Island Developing** - Fiji - Timor-Leste (2)	**Upper-middle** - People's Republic of China - Malaysia (2) **High** - Republic of Korea (1)	**High** - Malaysia (1) **Very High** - Republic of Korea (1)	**Less than 10 million** - Fiji - Mongolia - Timor-Leste (3)

2.4 Data Collection Methodologies

In order to assess the applicability of the suggested analytical framework to countries in Asia and the Pacific region, a series of methodological steps have been taken including the 1) web measurement analysis, and 2) calculation of framework index. Additionally, an 3) online based country expert survey and focus group interviews in selected countries were conducted in order to draw out deeper policy insights from the profiled countries. The following presents the methodologies used to conduct these three steps, which, combined together, will be used for the analysis in the next chapter with an aim to serve as a pilot assessment to evaluate the feasibility and validity of the Analytical Framework under a broader context.

2.4.1   Web Measurement Analysis

Unlike the two other dimensions of the suggested analytical framework, *Telecommunication Infrastructure* and *Capacity Development*, raw data for the third dimension, *Online Service for Women*, cannot be directly drawn or calculated from international statistical sources. In order to create index values for this category, a separate Web Measurement Analysis was conducted for the website of the national gender machineries of 11 selected countries. In particular, the analysis reveals the type and scope of e-Government services for women, the effectiveness of the provision of content and services reflecting women's needs and interests, and the provision of opportunities for women to participate in the policy making process.

The Web Measurement Analysis methodology was adopted from EGDI. The functionality of a national gender machinery website has been evaluated and scored according to the following four aspects: 1) information dissemination and outreach, 2) access and usability, 3) service delivery capability, and 4) citizen participation and interconnectedness ([Table 5).

The first category looks at features that would be likely to appear on an official gender ministry website, i.e. visions and mission statement of the ministry, organizational structure, news and updates, archives of legal and policy references, and the existence of personal account for individual users. The second category is concerned with feature that would assist easy and convenient access and use of the website contents and services including but not limited to search, contact addresses, multimedia, multiple language support, and electronic payment and security features. The third category addresses the e-service delivery capacity of the website. For example, downloadable or printable forms, job opportunities, email alerts and online-based transactions and services such as e-learning. The fourth category is concerned with factors related to citizen participation and interconnectedness. These features include, for example, the existence of e-Participation policy, listings of participatory activities, and participatory tools such as polls, feedback forms, bulletin boards, blogs and SNS.

Assessment was conducted based on a total score of features available at the national gender machinery website under examination. For binary questions, a country scored 1 when the website has a specific feature, while a score of 0 was given when the feature is absent. For list type questions, a normalized z score was used by comparing a total number of relevant features from a website with the average score of 11 countries. Then, the total scores for each of the four aspects were weighted accordingly, and summed up following the calculation method used for the EGDI.[11] The figures below illustrate the procedure conducted to calculate online service score and categorization of development stage.

---

[11] The 2012 EGDI Online Service Index value is presented in normalized forms to facilitate comparisons across countries. However, the index value of this research did not follow this final normalization process for the following reasons, since the limited number of country samples used for this research does not merit country comparison in a ranking format.

[Table 5] Criteria for Web Measurement Analysis of National Gender Machinery[12]

Aspects	No.	Criteria	Type
Information Dissemination/ Outreach (Emerging Stage)	1	Existence of ministerial websites pertaining to gender equality or any institute performing equivalent functions	Binary
	2	Existence of a portal for women in addition to the ministerial website	Binary
	3	Existence of an e-Government section under the ministry website	Binary
	4	Sources of archived information	Binary
	5	News and/or updates on government policies relating to women	Binary
	6	Access to back-office applications i.e. internal email system, information management system for employees	Binary
	7	Information concerning responsible government officials	Binary
	8	Personal accounts/profiles of women, with the objective of enhancing dialogue between government and women	Binary
	9	Information for citizens/women on how to use the website	Binary
Access/Usability (Enhanced Stage)	10	Search feature	Binary
	11	"Contact us" feature	Binary
	12	Audio and video features	Binary
	13	Multiple languages available	Binary
	14	Use of wireless technology to send messages to mobile phones or devices	Binary
	15	Security (secure link) feature available/indicated	Binary
	16	Electronic signature feature	Binary
	17	Online payment by credit, debit, or other card methods	Binary
	18	E-mail sign-up option, either as a formal list-serv or simply for news items	Binary
	19	Existence of features to enable access for people with disabilities	Binary
Service Delivery Capability (Transactional Stage)	20	Downloadable/printable forms	Binary
	21	Online forms	Binary
	22	Job opportunities	Binary
	23	Online transactions/ services (number of services normalized across countries)	List
	24	E-mail alerts for e-Participation	Binary
	25	Real Simple Syndication (RSS) use for e-Participation	Binary
	26	Set turnaround time for government to respond to submitted forms	Binary
Citizen Participation/ Interconnectedness (Connected Stage)	27	e-Participation policy or mission statement	Binary
	28	Calendar listings of upcoming participatory activities	Binary
	29	Archived information about past participatory activities	Binary
	30	Participatory tools to obtain public/women's opinion (number of tools across countries/ up-to 4 points)	List
	31	Provision for publishing the results of user feedback	Binary
	32	Archive of responses by government to citizen's questions	Binary

---

[12] Adopted from the UN E-Government Survey Online Service Index (2012)

[Figure 5] Sample Calculation of Online Service Score

Aspects	No	Criteria	Score	Weighted Score
Information dissemination/ Outreach **Emerging Stage Relative Weight: 7%**	1	Existence of ministerial websites	1	
	2	Existence of a portal for women	1	
	3	Existence of an e-Government section	1	
	4	Sources of archived information	1	
	5	News and/or updates on government policies relating to women	1	
	6	Access to back-office applications	1	
	7	Information concerning responsible government officials	1	
	8	Personal accounts/profiles of women	1	
	9	Information for citizens/women on how to use the website	1	
		Sub Total (Percentage Score)	**9 (90%)**	**7%**
Access/Usability **Enhanced Stage Relative Weight: 24%**	10	Search feature	1	
	11	"Contact us" feature	1	
	12	Audio and video features	1	
	13	Multiple languages available	1	
	14	Use of wireless technology	1	
	15	Security (secure link) feature available/indicated	1	
	16	Electronic signature feature	1	
	17	Online payment	0	
	18	E-mail sign-up option	1	
	19	Existence of features to enable access for people with disabilities	1	
		Sub Total	**9 (90%)**	**21.6%**
Service Delivery Capability **Transactional Stage Relative Weight: 30%**	20	Downloadable/printable forms	1	
	21	Online forms	1	
	22	Job opportunities	1	
	23	Online transactions/ services	4	
	24	E-mail alerts for e-participation	1	
	25	Real Simple Syndication (RSS) use for e-participation	1	
	26	Set turnaround time for government to respond to submitted forms	1	
		Sub Total	**10 (100%)**	**30%**
Citizen participation/ Interconnectedness **Connected Stage Relative Weight: 39%**	27	E-participation policy or mission statement	1	
	28	Calendar listings of upcoming participatory activities	1	
	29	Archived information about past participatory activities	1	
	30	Participatory tools to obtain public/women's opinion	4	
	31	Provision for publishing the results of users feedback	1	
	32	Archive of responses by government to citizen's questions	1	
		Sub Total	**9 (100%)**	**39%**
		Web Measurement Score		**0.98**

Source: EGDI 2012

[Figure 6] Country Scores for Online Service for Women

Country	Online Service for Women Index (in order of decreasing value)	Stage I %	Stage II %	Stage III %	Stage IV %	Stage
Relative weight of Stages		7%	24%	30%	39%	
Republic of Korea	0.98	100%	90%	100%	100%	Connected
India	0.76	78%	50%	80%	89%	Transactional
Malaysia	0.74	67%	60%	90%	72%	Transactional
People's Republic of China	0.47	56%	50%	60%	33%	Enhanced
Viet Nam	0.44	56%	50%	30%	50%	Enhanced
Philippines	0.42	44%	40%	40%	44%	Enhanced
Mongolia	0.34	56%	50%	10%	39%	Enhanced
Indonesia	0.34	56%	50%	30%	22%	Enhanced
Bangladesh	0.23	44%	30%	20%	17%	Emerging
Timor-Leste	0.17	44%	50%	0%	6%	Emerging
Fiji	0.11	44%	50%	0%	0%	Emerging

2.4.2   Calculation of Framework Index

One of the primary objectives of this report is to explore factors that may contribute to increasing the level of e-Government readiness to promote gender equality in the public sector. The calculation of e-Government Readiness for Gender Equality as presented in the table below serves as a first step in this endeavor, as the index values provide a comparable data to assess the country's preparedness according to the three key dimensions. The calculation was conducted based on the Analysis Framework and data source enrolment as identified in Chapter 2. In addition, the graphical overview of index value according to the three key dimensions of e-Government Readiness for Gender Equality offers a quick tool to assess the strengths and weaknesses of a country's standing in a regionally comparable form.

[Figure 7] E-Government Readiness for Gender Equality by Country

Country	E-Government Readiness for Gender Equality Index	Sub Indexes		
		Dimension 1: Telecommunication Infrastructure	Dimension 2: Capacity Development	Dimension 3: Online Service for Women
Bangladesh	0.29	0.10	0.54	0.23
People's Republic of China	0.44	0.28	0.57	0.47
Fiji	0.293	0.24	0.37	0.11
India	0.42	0.14	0.39	0.76
Indonesia	0.33	0.20	0.47	0.34
Republic of Korea	0.71	0.80	0.38	0.98
Malaysia	0.52	0.40	0.45	0.74
Mongolia	0.39	0.22	0.62	0.34
Philippines	0.47	0.23	0.76	0.42
Timor-Leste	N/A	N/A	N/A	0.17
Viet Nam	0.448	0.30	0.53	0.44
Group Average	0.42	0.30	0.46	0.45

The calculation of the index, again, followed the broad guidelines used for the EGDI. Mathematically, the index is a weighted average of three scores on the three key dimensions of e-Government, namely: development status of telecommunication infrastructure, gender equality in the human capital, and the scope and quality of online services for women. The formula is as follows: ($\frac{1}{3}$ * Telecommunication Infrastructure index) + ($\frac{1}{3}$ * Capacity Development index) + ($\frac{1}{3}$ * Online Service for Women index).

Using the readiness index, the illustrative comparison of sub-index scores in three criteria may help decision-makers find the strengths and weaknesses of their respective country progress in gender inclusion in e-Government. In order to filter out the 'gender' impact of the e-Government index, the newly created e-Government Readiness for Gender Equality Index value of each country was compared against the EGDI 2012. As shown in the figure below, most of the profiled countries exhibited lower level of normalized scores – readiness – when gender factor was considered. With this measure, policy makers can gain a useful overview as to where they stand in embracing gender issues in e-Government.

[Figure 8] Gender Impact in e-Government

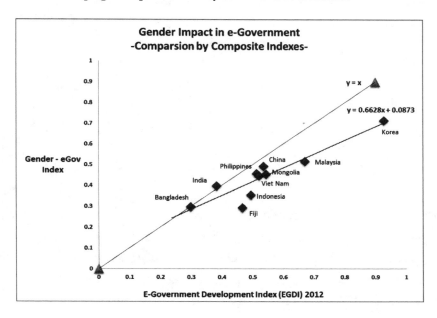

For example, People's Republic of China, India and Viet Nam in [Figure 8] have scored greater in online service for women index, which was calculated based on the web measurement analysis from the previous chapter, in comparison to the national e-Government initiatives in general – exhibiting a strong online service capacity for women through their national gender machinery websites. On the other hand, many other countries plotted below the y=x axis display a gender gap in the online service capacity.[13]

It is noted that due to the limited scope of this research, the index value calculation has to be conducted only for the 11 researched countries and consequently, generalization and replication of this framework to the worldwide level is not readily possible. Particularly, unlike the two other sub-indices in Telecommunication Infrastructure and Capacity Development where internationally comparable values can be easily drawn out, data for Online Service for Women, which was conducted through a web measurement analysis of national gender machinery, was newly created by the research team. However, even partial regional comparison may provide useful information helping governments identify their e-Government priorities and here lies the unique contribution of this research.

---

[13] When combined with the threshold of global mean score in online service capacity from EGDI, the plotting space provides a 2 by 2 matrix where countries can be grouped into four categories, depending on a country's general online service capacity and existing gender gap. Using this country grouping method, more targeted policy recommendations can be brought about. Chapter 4 will provide further description on the country grouping.

2.4.3   Online Expert Survey

In order to supplement the findings of the analysis framework, an online-based policy survey and focus group interviews were conducted targeting the relevant experts from 11 selected countries. The survey aimed to measure the perceived effectiveness of a country's e-Government policies for greater gender equality. Additionally, the survey gauges the perceived readiness of institutional capacity – such as the ICT competitiveness of its human resources, commitment from top leaders, as well as the cross-governmental coordination mechanism.

The perception of policy effectiveness and institutional readiness was measured according to five topics including: 1) goals and perceived effectiveness of e-Government policies; 2) e-Government's stated impact on gender equality; 3) visual or conceptual obstacles to women's use of e-Government services; 4) gender policy priorities and; 5) activities promoted by websites of national gender machinery.

The survey participants for each country were initially identified using the inter-governmental cooperation channels, UN systems and professional networks in academia and NGOs encompassing broad areas related to the theme, including but not limited to gender, ICT/e-Government, and public administration. A total of 242 completed survey questionnaires were received by October 1, 2012 from 11 selected countries.[14] The following figure summarizes the characteristics of respondents by each country.

---

[14] The research team noted that given the number of responses received and the criteria that had been applied to the selection of countries, it should not be assumed that the results of the online survey are regionally representative. Nonetheless, the study sample can be viewed as a reasonable snapshot of countries in the region.

[Figure 9] Number of Survey Responses from Countries[15]

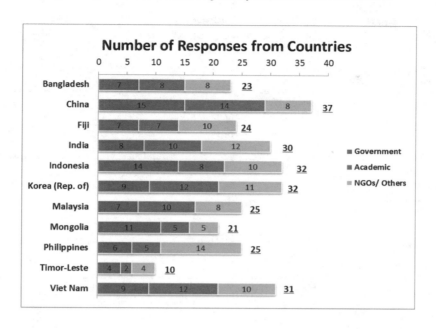

---

[15] Depending on the population size of the country, the minimum number of responses were set as below to be included in the analysis

Population Size*	Countries	Weight	Target Threshold
Over 1 billion	People's Republic of China, India	2	30
100 million – 1 billion	Indonesia, Bangladesh	1.5	23
10-100 million	Viet Nam, The Philippines, Republic of Korea, Malaysia	1.2	18
Less than 10 million	Mongolia, Timor-Leste, Fiji	1	15

31

The table below outlines the formation of the survey questionnaires.

[Table 6] Organization of Survey

Section	No.	Content
Policy goals of e-Government policies for women	1	ICT access
	2	ICT capacity building
	3	Linkage to e-Government
	4	Women's equal access to government services
	5	e-Participation
	6	Network building
	7	Online service development
	8	Gender advocacy
	9	Monitoring of gender impact
Perceived effectiveness of e-Government policies for women	10	ICT access
	11	ICT capacity building
	12	Linkages with e-Government
	13	Women's equal access to government services
	14	e-Participation
	15	Network building
	16	Online service development
	17	Gender advocacy
	18	Monitoring gender impact
Perceived impact of e-Government to promote gender equality	19	Overall contribution to gender equality in public sector
	20	Improved women's access to government services
	21	Delivery of online social services for women
	22	Strengthened the service quality of the Ministry of Gender
	23	Promoted women's participation in the political process
	24	Supported women parliamentarians
Obstacles to gender inclusion in e-Government	25	Sociocultural factors
	26	The rural and urban divide
	27	Income inequality between women and men
	28	Lack of language support
	29	Lack of content relevancy
	30	Different gender patterns of technology use
	31	Attitudes of women towards technology
	32	Lack of gender analysis in the telecom industry
	33	Lack of gender framework in public administration
Policy priorities for gender inclusion in e-Government	34	Identify women's e-Government service needs
	35	Design online public services reflecting women's needs
	36	Improve delivery of e-Government services for women
	37	Develop institutional/ staff capacity
	38	Build a stronger alliance with national e-Government strategy
	39	Monitor gender impacts of e-Government services

3. Country Profiles

3.1   Country Profiles

This section presents the profiles of 11 selected countries including Bangladesh, People's Republic of China, Fiji, India, Indonesia, Republic of Korea, Malaysia, Mongolia, the Philippines, Timor-Leste, and Viet Nam, regarding their degree of readiness of e-Government for gender equality. Each country profile is structured into four parts: 1) a brief description of the country's national gender machinery, 2) e-Government Readiness for Gender Equality Index values, 3) web measurement analysis of the national gender machinery website, and 4) the result of the expert survey on e-Government and gender policy.

[Table 7] Summary of Country Profiles

Country	Online Service Level	e-Gov Interactions				Key Features by Category			
		G2G	G2B	G2C	G2E	Info Dissemination	Use & Accessibility	Service Delivery	Citizen Participation
Bangladesh	Emerging			O	O	Org. info Legal info Publication Links News	Search Contacts Multimedia	N/A	Feedback
People's Republic of China	Enhanced	O		O	O	Org. info Legal info Publication Links News	Search Contacts Multimedia Email list	Forms Internal info – exchange system	Feedback Polls
Fiji	Emerging			O		Org. info Links	Search Contacts	Forms	N/A
India	Transactional		O	O	O	Org. info Legal info Publication Links News	Search Contacts Multimedia Email list	Forms Internal email system Online complaint/counseling system	Feedback Polls SNS links
Indonesia	Enhanced		O	O	O	Org. info Legal info Publication Links News	Search Contacts Multimedia Email list Language translation	Forms Internal email system Online library	Feedback Polls SNS links
Malaysia	Transactional	O		O	O	Org. info Legal info Publication Links News	Search Contacts Multimedia Email list RSS Access for disabled	e-learning Financial management for single parents Mammogram subsidy management Petition	Feedback Polls SNS
Mongolia	Enhanced			O	O	Org. info Legal info Publication Links News	Search Contacts Multimedia	Internal email system	Polls SNS links
The Philippines	Enhanced		O	O	O	Org. info Legal info Publication Links News	Search Contacts Multimedia Email list	Bidding system Recruitment system	Polls SNS (Box) BBS
Republic of Korea	Connected	O	O	O	O	Org. info Legal info Publication Links News User guide	Search Contacts Multimedia Email list Access for disabled Mobile connection Citizen's personal account Security	Women Net Service (Box) Women talent registration e-learning	Polls SNS links BBS Online petition(national portal) Citizen proposal Information disclosure request
Timor-Leste	Emerging			O	O	Org. info Links News Documents	Search Contacts Multimedia	N/A	N/A
Viet Nam	Enhanced			O		Org. info Links News Documents	Search Contacts Multimedia	N/A	Online petition

3.1.1   Bangladesh

The national machinery of gender equality in Bangladesh is the Ministry of Women and Child Affairs (MOWCA). MOWCA was established in 1978 to fulfill government commitments toward women's development. In the same year, the country-wide development plan recognized the unique needs of women and provided gender-disaggregated allocation programmes.

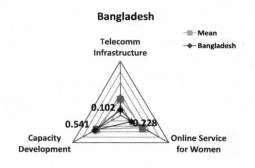

[Figure 10] Bangladesh: e-Government Readiness for Gender Equality

The MOWCA website is structured in four categories: 1) News and Updates, 2) Ministry Information, 3) Policy Archives and 4) Feedback. However, apart from text-based information dissemination, the website does not offer basic search features or support two-way communication. Under a separate feedback section, citizens can electronically submit an online form to the Ministry on general topics, but the feature supports only text submissions and citizens can not directly contact officials, who are responsible for a specific programme or project under the Ministry. The site offers one text-based service that lists job opportunities in the Ministry, which is a typical G2E interaction feature. However, the information is not up-to-date. Overall, online services and participatory channels are not yet available in the website and the service capacity is considered to be at the Emerging level.

Bangladesh displays a comparatively low level of readiness in all three dimensions of the index measures, as shown in Figure 12. Particularly, its telecommunication infrastructure readiness is one of the lowest out of the 11 countries surveyed, which warrants more policy efforts to focus on affordable and equitable telecommunication access for women.

[Table 8] Bangladesh: MOWCA Website Analysis

Ministry of Women and Child Affairs
Website: http://www.mowca.gov.bd
Language(s): English
Online Service Level: Emerging
Interactions Available
    ● G2C: Information dissemination for external users
    ● G2E: Internal email, Recruitments
Web Features
    ● Information Dissemination: Organization Information, Links, Press Release, Legislation/Acts, Publication
    ● Use & Accessibility: Search, Contacts, Multimedia
    ● Service Delivery: N/A
    ● Citizen Participation: Feedback

Gender Objectives and Impact of Current e-Government Programmes

To the question regarding the policy goals of e-Government for women, most of the responding experts replied (92%) that improving women's capacity of and access to ICT is very critical. Such result is notable as it shows that the experts from Bangladesh place a strong emphasis on the strategic use of ICT to promote women's inclusion in the knowledge-based society. Participants were asked to rate the effectiveness of the MOWCA website in disseminating relevant information to women and extending the outreach of the Ministry's activities. The review was generally positive, reflecting the belief that the site is useful for the provision of information. However, the data revealed two areas in which the experts thought the website fell short of expectations – interactive engagement with women through participatory measures (13%), and monitoring and evaluation of women's online usage (38%).

Areas for Future Efforts

The experts identified inter-agency monitoring of gender impact as a key aspect in promoting gender equality in public affairs. Interestingly, the MOWCA website provides achievement reports of a number of different agency programmes containing quantifiable gender-based outcome statistics – possibly indicating a national emphasis to strengthen gender monitoring across its public administration. Overall, experts ranked e-Government participation and advocacy as the least important, indicating that provision of expanded access and capacity building for women should come first in order to fulfill the potential of greater participation.

When asked to identify the top two policy priorities, respondents from Bangladesh identified the importance of needs assessment and service delivery. One reason for these selections is that Bangladesh is at the initial stage of the national ICT promotion and e-Government development, as shown in the low score from the telecom infrastructure dimension of the framework, and policy priorities are commonly clustered around the needs assessment and service development.

The selection of the two tasks, which are usually conducted at the beginning of a policy development cycle, echoes with some of the recommendations suggested by the survey participants that "e-Government should be a means to an end" and "ICT can help deliver the programmes to more women."

Summary

Considering the still emerging level of e-Government presence in gender development area, the result of the policy survey from experts in Bangladesh revealed that basic ICT capacity building and provision of ICT access should be a priority to the government's effort. The experts also replied that overall, the presence of MOWCA website as a focal point of women-specific information services contributed to increasing gender equality in public service. Considering the generally low-level of website capacity as examined above, such appreciation may indicate the participants' perceived importance of online presence. However, the experts did not agree (72%) that it has contributed to providing opportunities for women to be involved in public decision making, indicating that its performance as a proactive participatory measure is not yet satisfactory.

Box 3

Info Lady, a solution for rural access to e-Government, Bangladesh

In Bangladesh, lack of access to key information services and entitlements often lead to exclusion and disempowerment of marginalized communities. In order to connect marginalized population to livelihood information and knowledge systems at their doorsteps, an innovative model of ICT-based rural women entrepreneurship was developed by D.Net (Development Research Network) Bangladesh. The "Info Lady" model aims to ensure access to information for all especially women and disabled in the community, create self-employment among rural educated women, and build a viable business model for poor communities with low cost ICTs.

As part of the "Info Lady" initiative, an educated rural woman receives specialized training and travels to remote areas by bicycle to offer variety of ICT-based and other services at the door-step of the rural community she lives in. An info lady carries a range of ICTs including a netbook computer with webcam, internet modem, headphone, digital camera, and a mobile phone as well as basic medical equipment such as pregnancy kit, blood pressure monitor, and sugar testing kit. Info Ladies offer services to various target groups including pregnant women, housewives, farmers, children, adolescent girls, and unemployed youths.

Besides helping sustainable economic development, Info Lady is an effective e-governance tool as well. For instance, Info Ladies has been found to be very effective for disseminating information in areas such as pension, vulnerable group development, handicap assistance etc. The database in their laptops enables Info Ladies to provide answers and solutions to the most common problems faced by people in villages. Help line service, commercial phone service, photography, livelihood information and knowledge service, voice call service, video, and internet-based information service are among the services provided by an info lady.

The info Ladies are selected carefully from the locality using a rigorous selection criteria and their capacities are developed through various training activities. They receive technical training on operating laptop, internet, and other equipment; they also receive training in how to mobilize people and in health services such as blood tests, pregnancy tests, sugar tests, blood pressure measurement, weight measurement etc.

The Info lady profession was not easy to establish and there were many challenges along the road. In the beginning, the villagers were all skeptical about the Info Lady profession and it took them a while to accept, understand, and utilize the services provided by an Info Lady. Another major cause of concern was the personal safety of these women and their equipment- aproblemD.Net resolved by ensuring political support and building rapport with local NGOs.

Info Lady systematically creates a self-sustainable knowledge networks in rural Bangladesh. In rural and remote areas of Bangladesh, where women with basic education have few opportunities for gainful employment, "Info Lady" project has marked a paradigm shift in women's empowerment by creating information-based self-employment. It also created a 'trusted pathway' for rural women to access services that were previously denied to them. They are not passive beneficiaries but are now part of a trusted network that has fellow women who offer a range of ICT-based information services to improve their lives.

Encouraged by the successful completion of the pilot phase, in 2010, D.Net undertook a five year development plan to promote and expand the Info Lady model across the country through a 'Franchise Model. As part of this initiative, Info lady recently signed a tripartite financial agreement among D.Net, Fair Price International private Limited and National Bank Limited. Under this franchise model, D.Net will act as the knowledge partner while Fair Price International private Limited will work on implementation.

The sustainability of Info lady program is inextricably linked to program sustainability. Beyond commercial voice services, info lady offers a range of other value-added services which are in constant demand. The program constantly adds various essential services and updates other important services that are critically important to target groups.

Among the key lessons learnt, it is well-documented that success of the Info Lady program is heavily dependent on the Info lady's performance and motivation to her work. Locally relevant content is another crucial element to make available information more useful.

However, for program replication, it is also essential to identify appropriate services for each community since information need might vary from place to place. It is also critical to ensure transparency in the operational chain to create trust-based partnership among players.

In rural Bangladesh, where traditions are often rigid, Info ladies have enriched rural women's life by ensuring their access to information. The Info Lady project has proven to be an effective and sustainable business model — empowering not only the people it is designed to serve, but also the women who deliver the services.

Address: 6/8 Humayun Road, Block-B,
Mohammadpur, Dhaka-1217.
Ph: +88 02 9131424, +88 02 8124976
E-mail: info@dnet.org.bd
http://infolady.com.bd/

3.1.2　People's Republic of China

The National Working Committee on Children and Women (NWCCW) under the State Council is the central agency in People's Republic of China that governs women's empowerment. It was founded in 1990 as an official coordination mechanism approved by the State Council, and comprises members from the central party, ministries, commissions and NGOs. It is responsible for coordinating and promoting relevant government departments to implement laws and regulations, as well as policy-related measures concerning women and children and to develop women and children's cause.

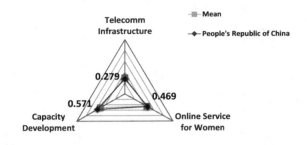

[Figure 11] People's Republic of China: e-Government Readiness for Gender Equality

Overall, the extent of online services from the NWCCW website remains at an Enhanced stage. The main features of the web service address information dissemination objectives, such as documentations on policy and regulations, news updates and research publications. It provides a small number of multimedia resources through embedded video streaming service from a third-party provider, which is an indigenous social networking service in People's Republic of China. With regard to the interactivity features, basic online polls, newsletter subscription, feedback forms and internal search engine are available.

[Table 9] People's Republic of China: NWCCW Website Analysis

National Working Committee on Children and Women
Website: http://www.nwccw.gov.cn/
Language(s): Chinese, English
Online Service Level: Enhanced
Interactions Available
- G2G:Internal Information Exchange Platform
- G2C: Information dissemination for external users
- G2E: Internal email, Recruitments

Web Features
- Information Dissemination: Organization Information, Links, Press Release, Legislation/Acts, Publication
- Use & Accessibility: Search, Contacts, Multimedia, Email subscription
- Service Delivery: Downloadable forms, Internal Info. Exchange system
- Citizen Participation: Feedback, polls, survey

National Policies on ICT/ e-Government Development for Women

When asked to identify which entity currently exercises the strongest influence over policy initiatives to promote women's access to ICT / e-Government, most of the participants mentioned the NWCCW (58%), followed by the national ICT machinery. Several participants specifically mentioned the China National Programme for Women's Development (2011-2020) (Box). The majority of participants (50%) recognize that NWCCW should continue playing the leadership role for a greater gender inclusion in e-Government.

Gender Objectives and Impact of Current e-Government Programmes

Respondents pointed out that promotion of women's participation in the decision-making process should be the most important goal of gender inclusion initiative in e-Government (74%). Other important objectives include ensuring women's equal opportunities to access public service (71%) and enhancing women's ICT capacity (71%). Regarding the impact of current programmes, participants' evaluation was close to neutral in all areas including infrastructure access, capacity building, public service outreach, participation and gender advocacy. In particular, the survey revealed that the national gender website is not satisfactory toward the goals of delivering useful and relevant online services for women (66%) and interactively engaging with its constituencies (66%).

Areas for Future Efforts

Regarding the obstacles to gender inclusion initiatives in e-Government, participants mentioned that the lack of national data on women's ICT use is critical (80%). The result supports a finding that has emerged across all eleven researched countries in this report, that the missing gender-ICT data is a significant roadblock in the path. When asked to identify policy priorities for future efforts, the most number of participants mentioned that it is critical to design e-Government programmes reflecting actual needs of women (69%) and identify women's service needs (56%).

Summary

Overall, the policy survey revealed that a key to effective online service creation and delivery lies in measuring women's e-Government needs and use. In this regard, a majority of participants emphasized the leading role, which the national gender mechanism should play across the government, is to avail itself of collecting relevant data for the design, development, delivery and monitoring of women-focused e-Government initiatives.

Box 4

China National Programme for Women's Development (2011-2020)

The China National Programme for Women's Development is an example of national level gender empowerment policy that includes women's equitable access to ICT as one of the strategic goals. The policy is spearheaded by the National Working Committee on Children and Women, and specifically mentions its goal to "improve women's use of media for access to knowledge and information," and to "support and promote the remote rural women who are restricted by poverty, mobility and disability by using media and communication technologies."

People's Daily Online (Aug 8, 2011)
http://politics.people.com.cn/h/2011/080
8/c226651-2249608525.html

3.1.3   Fiji

The Ministry of Women, Culture and Social Welfare (MWCSW) is the primary of the Fiji government that governs policies influencing women. Of the three departments under the Ministry, the Department of Women holds the responsibility to carry out a number of women development programmes and provide policy and advisory support to other ministries as well as to women groups.

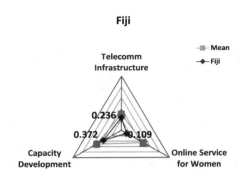

[Figure 12] Fiji: e-Government Readiness for Gender Equality

The homepage of MWCSW provides what is typical of an Emerging level web presence. The website is structured in four main categories, including Overview of the Ministry, Departmental Information, Statutory Bodies and Links, and Contact Details. The Overview section presents the vision and mission of the Ministry in a simple text form. Departmental Information offers more features through static online links on the page, such as statistics and downloadable forms for application to gender programmes offered by the Ministry. The site provides a link to the national e-Government Portal, the GOVNET, which is an initiative strongly supported by the Fiji government under the Roadmap for Democracy & Sustainable Socio-Economic Development (RDSSED) 2009-2014.

The readiness indicator reflects the emerging status of ICT development in Fiji with below the mean level of telecommunication infrastructure in the country. Considering the still emerging level of Fiji's e-Government development, key actions should be taken in focusing on improving women's access to telecommunication infrastructure and ICT capacity at the grassroots level, as well as raising awareness of the senior officials in the MWCSW to consider the potential of greater ICT application in its gender administration.

[Table 10] Fiji MWCSW Website Analysis

Ministry of Women, Culture and Social Welfare
Website: http://www.women.fiji.gov.fj/
Language(s): English
Online Service Level: Emerging
Interactions Available
• G2C: Information dissemination for external users
Web Features
• Information Dissemination: Ministry Information, Links
• Use & Accessibility: Search, Contacts
• Service Delivery: Downloadable forms
• Citizen Participation: NA

National Policies on ICT/ e-Government Development for Women

Most of the respondents (83%) replied that they are not aware of the national ICT policies aimed at promoting ICT empowerment for women. Participants showed a diverse spectrum of perceptions regarding the inter-agency coordination addressing women's ICT/e-Government empowerment. To the question, which entity in the government currently holds the strongest influence and ownership over the topic of women's inclusion in e-Government, the most number of participants (33%) replied central agencies such as Fiji Government Online and Fiji e-Government Portal, independent departments under the Government of Fiji, followed by the Department of Information Technology and Computing Services.

Gender Objectives and Impact of Current e-Government Programmes

Participants answered that the most important objective of gender inclusion in e-Government is to promote women's participation in the public decision-making process (83%), followed by ensuring an equitable access to public service (75%). However, the perceived effectiveness of government efforts towards these goals was not satisfactory overall, particularly showing the lowest perceived effectiveness on its capacity to deliver online services for women (50%). Reflecting the result, respondents evaluated that the performance of the national gender ministry's website is not satisfactory due to its slow update cycle, limited scope of information service, and inconvenient interface for users.[16] Key suggestions for improvement included incorporating training and empowerment strategies through collaborations with tertiary institutions that are equipped with ICT resources, improving the technical capabilities of services providers, and building a link to the national e-Government site.

Areas for Future Efforts

When asked to identify challenges in promoting the topic, most of the respondents pointed out the lack of inter-agency coordination across the government (59%) and the absence of key information and analysis on the use of ICT by women (73%). Respondents' answers to the areas of future policy development also reflected this result. The collection of gender-disaggregated national statistics was considered as a priority (58%), followed by the need to identify women's ICT and e-Government service needs (50%).

Summary

Combined together, the result indicates that at the initial stage of e-Government application for women, the priority should be set to understand the current status of women's ICT access, skills, and use, in order to draw out relevant policy alternatives.[17] Respondents also emphasized the need to build a strong tie between women's e-development and national ICT / e-government

---

[16] Excerpted from written suggestions of respondents.

[17] One of the respondents pointed out that according to the inter-governmental circular in 2010, gender-disaggregated data should be incorporated in all policy documents in Fiji and as such, it is recommended to adopt a central data and information management system that reflects gender statistics and data.

strategy, again, as one of the key steps to be taken at the early stage of e-Government application for gender administration.

3.1.4   India

The Ministry of Women and Child Development (MWCD) is the central Ministry for the advancement of women in India. The National Commission for Women (NCW), an apex national level organization under the MWCD has the direct mandates for promoting and protecting the interests of women.[18]

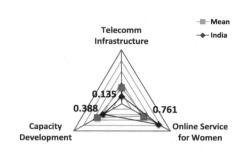

India

[Figure 13] India: e-Government Readiness for Gender Equality

The NCW website is reaching an advanced Enhanced stage of online service development. The website is structured in five main categories, including Overview of the Commission, document archives, and a notice board for public and business, participation avenues, and programme pages. Several noticeable public participation initiatives are presented. First, the site offers a *Complaint Online* section, where citizens can file complaints or consultation requests via an interactive web form and check the progress online. Also under the progress reports section, the email address of the designated officer is provided for the public to send suggestions. The website offers links to the national government portal, national grievance registration system, as well as other websites of relevant government agencies and independent commissions.

[Table 11] India: MWCD Website Analysis

Ministry of Women and Child Development **Website**: http://wcd.nic.in/   **Language(s)**: English, Hindi **National Commission for Women** **Website**: http://ncw.nic.in/   **Language(s)**: English **Online Service Level**: Transactional **Interactions Available** • G2C: Information dissemination for external users • G2B: Tender/Auction/Purchase notice • G2E: Internal email, Recruitments **Web Features** • Information Dissemination: Organization Information, Links, Press Release, Legislation/Acts, Publication • Use & Accessibility: Search, Contacts, Subscription, Multimedia, Multiple language • Service Delivery: Downloadable forms, Internal email system, Online Complaint/Counseling System • Citizen Participation: Feedback (an external link to national public grievance portal), Polls, Survey

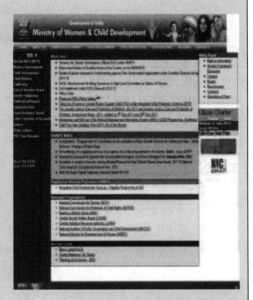

---

[18] Both organizations are recognized as representatives of national gender mechanisms by the UN Women. For the purpose of the study, NCW has also been considered for review, which specializes in gender issues of the two main beneficiary groups of MWCD and serves as a gateway to public online services for women.

The current status of online service for women exhibits an advanced capacity compared to other areas of the readiness indicator. Considering the relatively weak telecommunication infrastructure as shown in the Framework analysis, and the vast size of the country, key actions should be taken to improve the last-mile delivery of online services to women in localities. For example, a mobile-based extension of the current Complaint Online system can be considered, taking into account the relatively high penetration rate of mobile phones in remote areas of India[19].

National Policies on ICT/ e-Government Development for Women

Most participants (55%) identified that the Department of Electronics and Information Technology (DEIT) has a specialized policy and programmes to develop e-literacy of women under its Common Service Center (CSC) initiative (Box). Also, the majority of respondents (60%) recognized that DEIT has the strongest influence over current ICT and e-Government initiatives for women as a subgroup of its beneficiaries. However, the most number of participants (40%) replied that the MWCD should play a leading role in future policy developments for women's inclusion in e-Government, indicating a call for a greater domain-specific expertise to be incorporated in the policy development process.

Box 5

Women Digital Literacy Scheme, National e-Government Plan of India

The programme is conducted in part of India's national e-Government plans, implemented by DEIT under its Common Services Centers Scheme (CSC). The scheme leverages on the existing certification programme for community access point operators and applies the proven concept to address rural women's ICT access and capacity divide.

http://csc.gov.in/index.php?option=com_content&view=article&id=180&Itemid=347

Gender Objectives and Impact of Current e-Government Programmes

Respondents replied that e-government should in priority aim at improving women's ICT access (86%) and enhancing women's ICT capacity (79%), followed by online service delivery (66%) and promotion of women's participation in decision-making (60%). The result underscores that improving women's ICT access and capacity, cannot and should not be considered separately from the general objectives of e-Government, as the two are the most fundamental prerequisites for e-Government inclusion. When asked to evaluate the effectiveness of current programmes, the most participants appreciated women's improved access to information (64%). Online service delivery in terms of its relevance (42%) and quality (35%) was considered as the most unsatisfactory, indicating respondents' higher standard expected from the national gender website. Respondents suggested that online services via national gender mechanism should provide more than just information and embrace more interactive transaction services. e-Service development in family welfare, career development, and education/training were suggested as areas where e-Government application can provide the most advantage.

---

[19] Internet and Mobile Association of India (IAMAI) and IMRB report *Internet in Rural India (2012)* stated that mobile phones are fast emerging as an important point of internet access in rural India. As of June 2012, there were 3.6 million mobile internet users in India, a growth of 7.2 times from 0.5 million in 2010.

Areas for Future Efforts

When asked to identify challenges to gender inclusion in e-Government, more than 90% of the respondents pointed out the low relevancy of contents and information to specific needs of women (93%). Considering the size of the country, developing a programme catered to the different livelihood conditions women face is a key factor in determining the efficiency of any online service. Participants also identified the lack of ICT knowledge among government staff (86%) and the unavailability of gender statistics on ICT usage (86%) as major challenges. It is interesting to note that the participants in India perceived obstacles in the programme design stage of the policy development cycle to be more significant than those in the implementation stage, such as public administration framework and inter-agency coordination across ministries. The result again may support the finding that the domain knowledge in gender empowerment should be well-incorporated in the e-Government plans.

Summary

Overall, the result of the policy survey in India revealed that the national gender machinery should play a greater role in promoting women's inclusion in e-Government; programme knowledge in gender development should be more closely incorporated with e-government initiatives, in order to improve the relevancy and efficacy of the programme.

Box 6

ICT Growth Effect on Women's Empowerment in India

In all, India's ICT sector has played – and continues to play – a pivotal role in bridging the gender divide in the country's workforce by helping to overcome biases against women and girls in general, and women with rural or uneducated backgrounds in particular. It has not only been at the forefront in Asia in offering women access to the country's ICT sector through numerous educational and practical, hands-on, pro-gender initiatives (like encouraging girls and women to enter computer and ICT engineering courses; offering special 'pick-and-drop' taxi facilities; establishing anti-sexual harassment committees; providing maternity leave during pregnancy and creating exclusive web portals for females, etc.), it has also achieved one of the highest gender ratios of the general workforce (31 per cent in 2009) in the region and is making managerial positions open to women (20 per cent in 2009).

Excerpted from *A Bright Future in ICTs: Opportunities for new generation of women*, ITU, 2012. p.33.
Original Source:
Impact of IT-BPO Industry in India: A Decade in Review, pp. 12-13;
http://nasscom.in/upload/68924/Impact_Study_2010_Exec_Summary.pdf

Box 7

Mission Convergence (Samajik Suvidha Sangam), Delhi, India

Mission Convergence (MC) (or *Samajik Suvidha Sangam*), a flagship programme of the Delhi Government, was created in 2008 in order to improve governmental performance on the goal of poverty alleviation by integrating existing social security schemes and delivering them through a unified structure in a decentralized manner, with a parallel focus on empowering women through interventions in the areas of livelihood, health, non-formal education, and legal literacy.

Project Design
Starting from the premise that the main obstacle in advancing poverty alleviation in the National Capital Territory (NCT) of Delhi was inequity, rather than shortages in social sector spending (as pointed out in the 2006 Human Development Report for Delhi), the NCT government had come to the conclusion that the benefits of its various welfare schemes were not reaching the intended beneficiaries to a sufficient degree. The reasons for this were seen in low levels of awareness about available schemes and programmes among vulnerable households, as well as administrative challenges in adequately identifying and enrolling beneficiaries in the relevant in health, nutrition, education, social security, employment, and gender equity programmes. In order to break the mutually reinforcing cycle of inaccurate poverty estimates, unrealistic budget allocations, and the exclusion of the most marginalised, MC deployed a 'four-pronged strategy' consisting of:

1. Convergence of schemes (including a review & abolition of non-functioning ones);
2. Redefining poverty using new proxy indicators;
3. Partnership with civil society; and
4. Leveraging technology

Operational Structure of Mission Convergence (*Samajik Suvidha Sangam*)

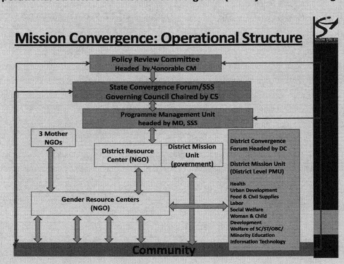

Gender Governance
The Mission Convergence project had its origins in the Women & Child Development department of NCT Delhi. Combined with the devolution of implementing authority to many women's groups on the ground, based on previous experiences with successful public-private partnership programmes for community outreach, this led to a sustained focus on women's needs. Community owned and partnered structures at fixed locations, called 'Gender Resource Centres' (GRCs) were set up and given the authority to serve as first points of contact for the community on all assistance programmes. Based on poverty mapping exercises, each centre serves an area of about 15,000 – 20,000 vulnerable households. Thus far, 104 GRCs have been set up in Delhi, along with 20 extension centres. The staff at each GRC consists of a Project Coordinator, a Project Officer, a VT instructor, a Help Desk assistant, an NFE instructor, a Community Mobilizer, and an accountant, with pharmacists, doctors, and lawyers present on a visiting basis.

Apart from facilitating access to general government schemes such as UID (universal identity cards), RSBY (health insurance), and PDS (subsidised food supplies available through the Public Distribution System), the GRCs offer a variety of specific so-called women empowerment and development programmes in areas such as in health, sanitation, nutrition, non-formal/bridge education, legal awareness & counselling, vocational training, SHG formation and microfinance activities, entrepreneurship, etc.

Rather than putting the onus on beneficiaries to potential beneficiaries to approach a particular government office for information about available assistance schemes, MC has reversed this process through the widespread use of community facilitators – using the networks established during the survey phase for the development of the vulnerability index – who bring the relevant information into the community on a regular basis, and thus establish a closer link between beneficiaries and the GRCs as local information and training hubs. This has reportedly been very successful in breaking down the barriers between poor communities and the government entities providing essential services to them, particularly with regard to enabling women to take advantage of services designed for them.

With regard to constraints and challenges, there was a realisation that the very process of automating the registration and service delivery apparatus across a variety of departments had brought with it particular challenges, as well as opportunities. While having largely succeeded in driving the process of convergence, officials admitted there had also been unforeseen practical difficulties, both of a technical nature (in terms of getting all departments to move to the same platform) and in terms of systemic resistance in view of the far-reaching implications of the administrative reorganisation underlying the MC reform efforts, since they often threatened the existing portfolios, budgets, and political influence of the concerned departments. One official pointed out that this had been an issue particularly at the level of the lower bureaucracy.

Project Outcomes

The project has succeeded in redefining dimensions of poverty in the Delhi NCT area, resulting in the extension of coverage in essential social welfare programmes to large numbers of previously excluded citizens (currently benefitting c. 1.2 million people annually).

In terms of replicability of the project in other cities and regions of India, the current Additional Director voiced the opinion that theoretically it should be possible to implement the same model elsewhere. He said that other, smaller cities, may in fact be better placed to implement such a project, given their smaller overall numbers of potential beneficiaries, as well as smaller numbers of migrants, which currently posed a big challenge in Delhi for establishing identity and confirming the eligibility of seasonally mobile beneficiaries. A good capacity level among the participating NGOs also helped make the project a success in Delhi. However, he noted that strong political support was indispensable in order to overcome administrative and bureaucratic obstacles at the implementation stage, and to ensure full cooperation of all involved departments, despite the far-reaching implications that such an initiative was likely to have on their respective budgets and political influence. Therefore, total commitment from the top, and visionary leadership, both in the political and bureaucratic spheres, were a crucial pre-condition. Other observers agreed that this was also the likely reason that 'convergence' had not made any particular headway at the national level in India yet.

Contact

Vishva Mohan, Additional Director: vishva.mohan@gmail.com
Brajnandan Kumar, Principal Consultant (IT): kumarbrajnandan@gmail.com

Website

http://www.missionconvergence.org/

Sources

Various internal documents obtained from MC staff

3.1.5 Indonesia

The Ministry of Women Empowerment and Child Protection (MWECP) is the primary organ in Indonesian government that governs policies affecting women. Notably, the MWECP established the "Development Policy on Improvement of Women's Lives 2010-2014", which sets out five priorities such as education, health, economic activities, political participation, and society and culture. The education priority includes activities designed to increase the number of women in science and technology, and to improve women's ICT access and use (JICA, 2010).

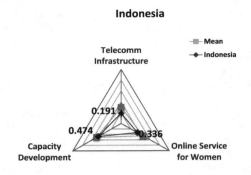

[Figure 14] Indonesia: e-Government Readiness for Gender Equality

Overall, the MWECP website has reached the Enhanced stage. The website is composed of five main categories including the Ministry Information, News and Updates, Data and Information Archive, online services including an Intranet portal and Suggestions and Questions. From a usability perspective, the website, originally offered in Bahasa Indonesia, provides a Google translation tool embedded at the Website navigation menu to reduce potential language barriers. In addition, it offers several online-based services for both citizens and MWECP staff. For example, a link to the Intranet service offers three category options including the Auction Announcement for public viewing, webmail for MWECP staff, and a link to a stand-alone online library service.

[Table 12] Indonesia: MWECP Website Analysis

Ministry of Women Empowerment and Child Protection	
Website: http://www.menegpp.go.id/ **Language(s)**: Bahasa Indonesia, English **Online Service Level**: Enhanced **Interactions Available** • G2C: Information dissemination for external users • G2B: Auction announcement • G2E: Internal email, Intranet library **Web Features** • Information Dissemination: Organization Information, Links, Press Release, Legislation/Acts, Publication • Use & Accessibility: Search, Contacts, Subscription, Multimedia, Language translation • Service Delivery: Downloadable forms, Internal email system, Online library • Citizen Participation: Feedback, Polls,, SNS link	

Gender Objectives and Impact of Current e-Government Programmes

Almost 80% of the respondents from Indonesia replied that e-Government should ensure women's access to ICT. Around 60% of the respondents identified that ensuring women's equal access to government services is also an important goal of e-Government promotion. The result displays a broad variety of participants' perceptions about the importance of streamlining e-Government service delivery for women, ranging from individual concerns about ICT capacity building to community level priorities regarding women's online networks, and further to more institutional level issues such as e-Government service integration and support of online participation channels.

Overall, almost 80% of the survey participants agreed that e-Government for women have contributed to gender equality in public sector. The majority of respondents replied that the e-Government provisions available via the MWECP website contributed to the online service quality of the Ministry (57%) and improved women's access to information on government services (54%). However, the participants generally expressed a lower level of confidence in the political empowerment aspect of e-Government; less than 40% of the participants replied that the MWECP website promoted women's participation in the political and democratic process and supported women parliamentarians.

Areas for Future Efforts

The majority of survey respondents replied that developing institutional and staff capacity to carry out e-Government programmes and services is the most important policy priority in Indonesia (62%). Respondents from Indonesia mentioned that the e-Government expertise in Indonesia is still in its beginning stage; thus it is critical to improve the awareness, within the institutional setting, about the efficiency and effectiveness that e-Government could potentially offer.

40% of the respondents stated that it was important to monitor the gender impact of e-Government. Given the national push for gender mainstreaming as mentioned on MWECP website, one of the important roles the MWECP plays is to ensure gender-responsiveness of government policies across all government agencies from design to implementation. As one of the respondents stated, e-Government can serve as an "effective means to coordinate and streamline gender-responsiveness monitoring" across different government agencies.

Summary

In sum, the result of the Indonesian policy survey revealed that the respondents agreed that the goal of e-Government is to serve as a tool to improve government service delivery for women. They perceived e-Government programmes for women to be effective means in improving gender equality in public service. However, the result also indicates that a distinction should be made between its role as service delivery and participatory channel.

3.1.6   Malaysia

The national mechanism for gender equality in Malaysia is the Ministry of Women, Family and Community Development (MWFCD). Among the four departments under the Ministry, the Department for Women's Development serves as the main hub for women's development, with its mission to integrate the needs of women into the mainstream and strengthen the family institution for increased social welfare.

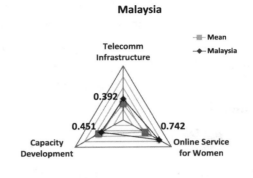

[Figure 15] Malaysia: e-Government Readiness for Gender Equality

The results of the MWFCD Web Measurement Analysis show that it has currently reached the Enhanced stage, and is in transition towards the Transactional level development. The website is organized into five main categories, including News and Updates, Policy Archives, Ministry Information, Services, and Citizen Participation. The first three categories focus on information dissemination and outreach, outlining the core work areas of the Ministry. It provides documentation, multimedia features, statistics about women and children's development and information about the Ministry's organizational structure. Under the Service category, the MWFCD website offers a number of links to information where citizens can directly receive online-based services including e-learning courses on reproductive health and online forms for financial assistance. The services provided include programmes for women's economic participation, education, health, and social inclusion child care. Additionally, usage statistics of such services are also available through a separate Transaction Statistics page.

[Table 13] Malaysia: MWFCD Website

Ministry of Women, Family and Community Development
Website: http://www.kpwkm.gov.my/
Language(s): Bahasa Malay, English
Online Service Level: Transactional
Interactions Available
• G2G: Internal information exchange platform
• G2C: Information dissemination for external users
• G2E: Internal email system, Recruitment
Web Features
• Information Dissemination: Organization Information, Links, Press Release, Legislation/Acts, Publication
• Use & Accessibility: Search, Contacts, Subscription, Multimedia, Multiple language, RSS, Access for disabled
• Service Delivery: E-learning, Financial management for Single Parents, Mammogram subsidy management, petition
• Citizen Participation: Feedback, Poll, SNS link, Survey

However, in order to make a transition from the third to the fourth and top phase of e-Government development, the MWFCD website would need to increase its capabilities to support seamless citizen engagement between the MWFCD website and the national e-Government portal (www.gov.my).

Gender Objectives and Impact of Current e-Government Programmes

In particular, the respondents considered ICT penetration a key goal of e-Government promotion for women. More than 70% of respondents identified that the enhancement of women's ICT capacity and access should be a top policy goal, compared to the relatively low level of importance placed on the policy integration, application development, and policy monitoring (29%). The access to technology, combined with the capacity to use technology, forms a multi-faceted challenge for women's ICT access. Considering that the ICT access serves as a basic requirement of women's e-Government usages, such emphasis on ICT penetration resonates with the overall policy priority in Malaysia.

Areas for Future Efforts

When asked to determine the two most pressing policy priorities to promote e-Government for gender equality, the greatest number of respondents stated that it was essential to identify women's e-Government service needs. Another notable result is the respondents' desire (43%) for the site to offer stronger linkage with other national e-Government strategies, and to provide a seamless, integrated service for its citizens.

The majority of experts responded that the MWFCD website has contributed to enhancing gender equality in the public sector (66%), particularly through the delivery of online social services and dissemination of information on government policies and programmes. Notably, the Ministry provides a variety of online-based services and content for women in reproductive health and social safety online. The respondents from Malaysia valued the role of ICT in improved information delivery, but they did not rank participatory engagement features very highly (29%).

Summary

Overall, the analysis of Malaysia exhibits a case of strong service outreach efforts geared towards providing gender-specific online services to women. Notably, such government efforts were perceived positively by experts, as they agreed that the current provision of e-Government contents and services via its Ministry website is effective in improving the public service delivery for women.

3.1.7 Mongolia

The National Committee on Gender Equality (NCGE) of Mongolia is the central organization in the Government of Mongolia with a mandate to achieve gender equality by supporting the formulation of national policy, and its implementation and evaluation.

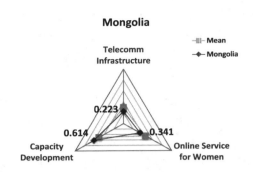

[Figure 16] Mongolia: e-Government Readiness for Gender Equality

The web analysis revealed that the website of NCGE currently provides an online service to its constituents at a late Emerging to an early Enhanced stage. The website is composed of five major areas of service, the organization information on its mandates, leadership and organization, documentations of laws and regulations pertaining to women's empowerment and protection, specific information on its programmes, a publication archive, and links to other government agencies and NGOs. However, most of the information available is simple and text-based, except for the publication archive where users can download PDF documents. No transaction services are available through the website, even though interactive features such as multimedia contents and external links to its SNS channels, including Facebook and Twitter, enhance the user experience. The website provides a user-friendly interface and an easy navigation compared to other emerging level websites.

Overall, the readiness indicator of Mongolia exhibits the need to exert more efforts to strengthen its online service capacity for women as shown in the Framework index. Considering that Mongolia's progress in both general e-Government online service capacity (UNDESA, 2012) and gender development is above the average of its peers in the same income group, the scope and quality of women-centered online services may make a significant leap with policy support.

[Table 14] Mongolia: NCGE Website Analysis

National Committee on Gender Equality
Website: http://gender.gov.mn   **Language(s)**: Mongolian, English
Online Service Level: Enhanced
Interactions Available
• G2C: Information dissemination for external users
• G2E: Internal email system
Web Features
• Information Dissemination: Organization Information, Links, News, Legislation/regulations, Publication, Links
• Use & Accessibility: Search, Contacts, Multimedia, Multiple language
• Service Delivery: Internal email system
• Citizen Participation: Poll, SNS (Facebook, Twitter)

National Policies on ICT / e-Government Development for Women

Regarding the question to identify national level policies to promote women's ICT/e-Government access, most of the survey participants answered that they are unaware of specific policies (60%). The most participants recognized that currently, Information Communications Technology and Post Authority (ICTPA) holds the strongest influence over the policy for women's ICT and e-Government empowerment (78%), whereas the same number of respondents answered that it should continue playing the leading role in this endeavor (78%). Combined together, the participants' perception over the leadership role assumed by the national ICT agency, ICTPA, may indicate that a clearly defined institutional framework has been set up and shared across the government departments.

Gender Objectives and Impact of Current e-Government Programmes

Respondents replied that e-government for gender equality should aim at building women's networks for a greater gender advocacy online (67%) and increasing women's participation in the public decision-making process (56%). The result shows that experts from Mongolia emphasized the use of e-Government as a tool of more efficient gender advocacy, compared to the objectives of improved ICT access or public service delivery. When asked to evaluate the effectiveness of current programmes, participants showed a positive review in general, noting that the policy has promoted women's participation in political and democratic process (83%) and improved women's access to information on government services (77%). However, their evaluation of the NCGE website as a women's gateway to e-Government was unsatisfactory. The perceived effectiveness of online service that is delivered through the website was particularly low as more than the majority of the respondents rated its quality as below average (61%), indicating respondents' higher standard for service delivery features. Participants suggested that the website should become more service-oriented in terms of its scope and variety, and move beyond the one-way dissemination of information.

Obstacles and Areas for Future Efforts

The most challenging obstacles perceived by the respondents included the lack of gender analysis in telecommunication industry (88%) and weak gender consideration in public administration in general (78%). The attention paid to the role of private sector, which was not found in other surveyed countries in this research, was significant. It is interesting to note that of those who identified the role of telecommunication industry, more than the majority (60%) were from the government. Considering the weak telecommunication infrastructure in Mongolia, the connectivity concern faced by women may have been reflected in this result.

Summary

In sum, the result of the policy survey in Mongolia indicated that the primary areas of e-Government in Mongolia include a greater gender advocacy channeled through e-Government as an important vehicle.

3.1.8 The Philippines

The Philippine Commission on Women (PCW) is the central agency for the promotion of women's rights in the Philippines. PCW was established in 1975 by a Presidential Decree and is responsible for planning, implementing, and assessing the National Plan for Women, as well as providing a cross-agency monitoring of gender-responsiveness.

The PCW website shows an Enhanced Stage of online service development for women. The website, which serves as the *"Gateway to Gender Development in the Philippines,"* provides

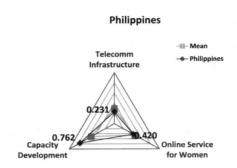

[Figure 17] The Philippines: e-Government Readiness for Gender Equality

information on women-related policy, governance, laws and regulations, and relevant documents. What is interesting is its G2B and G2E interactions that are available throughout the website. The interactions provide job and bidding opportunities from which users can view vacancies and bidding invitations, send postings to their personal email, obtain contact information of the hiring manager, and download application forms. Users can also share postings via Facebook. However, the website is limited in terms of its interactive features. Users cannot submit forms online or register to receive automatic updates on PCW activities. Currently, the features that allow a minimum level of two-way communication are the "Contact Us" form, which is a simple electronic form allowing users to send text-based messages to the webmaster, and a link to Facebook, where users can share links and add comments.

[Table 15] The Philippines: PCW Website Analysis

Philippine Commission on Women
Website: http://pcw.gov.ph/
Language(s): English
Online Service Level: Enhanced
Interactions Available
   ● G2C: Information dissemination for external users
   ● G2B: Bidding information
   ● G2E: Internal email system
Web Features
   ● Information Dissemination: Organization Information, Links, News, Legislation/regulations, Publication, Links
   ● Use & Accessibility: Search, Contacts, email subscription
   ● Service Delivery: Bidding / Recruitment system
   ● Citizen Participation: Poll, SNS (Facebook, Twitter), BBS

Considering the strong women's capacity value of the country as shown in the Framework Index, as well as the variety of programme information online, the PCW website seems ready to move towards the next level of e-Government development by spearheading its efforts to strengthen "transaction" and "interaction" with citizens and other organizations. This may include developing specialized public services and content, e-learning options, and electronic form submission systems. In addition to service delivery, the PCW homepage could better serve as a central platform for all gender-related issues. Two-way communication functionality such as forums, email alerts, and discussion boards are essential to provide a formal but open space for citizen participation.

The PCW website is not linked with other government agency websites. By creating these linkages, it would not only be advantageous to users, but also enable PCW to share content with other agencies and monitor gender equality integration on other sites. This can play an essential role in PCW's work as the central body that is responsible for the gender-responsiveness of public policies in the Philippines.

Gender Objectives and Impact of Current e-Government Programmes
The result of the policy survey in the Philippines revealed that the experts perceive that the national e-Government strategy for gender equality is effective (68%) and contributes to women's participation in the political and democratic process (60%). The experts identified a variety of e-Government and gender topics as equally important, from improving basic ICT access (68%) and capacity building for women (68%) to monitoring (60%) and advocating for gender-sensitive public service and participation (60%). Moreover, the experts highlighted "building women's online communities and networks" as an important goal of e-Government policy (60%).

In general, respondents valued the effectiveness of e-Government provisions very highly. Particularly, the respondents stated confidence in the system's contribution to the promotion of women's participation in political and government service (72%), as well as the availability of information on women-related government services (68%). Considering that the PCW website currently does not provide extensive participatory "online" space at the moment, the result may reflect the different process of policy development and deliberation unique to the context of the Philippines, which is conventionally considered as including participation from the civil society groups. Under this context where gender concerns are first gathered by the local grassroots networks in the civil society and then fed to the national mechanisms through civil society consultation, rooms for individual participation to the government processes may not warrant the urgent policy attention. As revealed in the Web Measurement Analysis, the PCW website provides an extensive list of partnering NGOs with which PCW jointly shapes policies and programmes for gender development. Combined with the fact that the survey participants chose the "building women's online network" as an important goal of the e-Government provision, the survey sheds light to an alternative model of e-Government development for women that utilizes the networking aspects of ICT to promote participation and improve service delivery (Box 8).

Areas for Future Efforts

The survey respondents replied that institutional (72%) and human resources readiness (68%) should be the top two policy priorities for gender-sensitive e-Government strategies. They stated that these are critical both within PCW and across other government agencies. One of the respondents from the government mentioned that the ICT capacity of programme managers should be improved to facilitate better design and delivery of online services for women.

Summary

Overall, the result of policy survey revealed that respondents highly valued the effectiveness of the e-Government provision in the country. While the level of e-Government sophistication still remains at the bottom second phase of the Web Measurement Index, the largely positive responses from the experts may have resulted from the strength of the Philippines' gender policy development and implementation records themselves, rather than the advancement of electronic delivery measures represented by e-Government per se.

Box 8

Social Networking Service, a new potential for Outreach, PCW, the Philippines

With the exponential growth of users of social networking services (SNS), the potential to use SNS for the promotion of online government services has been increasingly adopted. Facebook, the largest SNS has an increasingly number of users in developing countries, and more importantly, the portion of women users in the composition is significant. In response to this trend, an increasing number of national gender machinery in Asia and the Pacific region is adopting SNS in their public awareness programmes.

http://www.facebook.com/philippine.commission.on.women?ref=search

The PCW of the Philippines utilizes its Facebook page to provide additional information on its current programmes and activities as well as updates on the new legislation, notably the Magna Carta of Women. The Facebook page is actively managed and maintained by a designated staff member from the PCW, whose role includes answering inquiries received from Facebook users, and sharing video and audio links relevant to the gender development issues in the Philippines. Considering the limited technical sophistication at the level of emerging e-government development, such usage of social media as an alternative outlet to "receive" input as a participatory channel can be a viable option for many developing countries.

This social networking model also resonates with the gender pattern of Internet use. Even though specific results may differ across countries, recent research found that women tend to use the Internet more for social networking compared to men. In case of the Philippines, for example, the total number of Facebook users is about 27,000,000. This accounts for about 27% of its population and 90% of online population. Notably the male and female user ratio on Facebook is 48% to 52%, showing women's active usage of social networking compared to men. Another benefit of this networking model of e-government in the Philippines is the collection of links provided through the PCW website to relevant networks, such as local governments, relevant public institutes, academia, and private sector partners to the civil society.

3.1.9   Republic of Korea

The nodal organization for gender equality in Republic of Korea is the Ministry of Gender Equality and Family (MOGEF). The Ministry was established as part of the Presidential Commission on Women's Affairs in 1997, following the enactment of the Gender Discrimination Prevention and Relief Act. Since its inception, MOGEF has served as a central planning and coordination body for women's policies across the government.

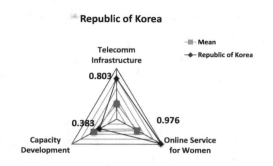

[Figure 18] Republic of Korea: e-Government Readiness for Gender Equality

E-Government services for women in Republic of Korea are at the Connected Stage. The MOGEF website serves as a platform through which women can access various e-Government services and contents that are specifically targeted for women's information needs, public service requirements and participatory channels.

Notable features from an accessibility and usability perspective include a mobile version of the website that supports the growing number of smart phone users in the country. From a service delivery perspective, the MOGEF website has developed several online-only features that can significantly increase public service provisions for women (Box).

[Table 16] Republic of Korea: MOGEF Website Analysis

Ministry of Gender Equality and Family
Website: http://mogef.go.kr/   **Language(s)**: Korean, English
Online Service Level: Connected
Interactions Available
- G2G: Internal information exchange platform
- G2C: Information dissemination for external users
- G2B: Bidding information
- G2E: Internal email system

Web Features
- Information Dissemination: Organization Information, Links, News, Legislation/regulations, Publication, Links, citizen's personal account, User guide
- Use & Accessibility: Search, Contacts, email subscription, Multiple language, Multimedia, Access for the disabled, Mobile connection, Security features
- Service Delivery: Women net (real-time mentoring and counseling), Women talent registration, e-learning
- Citizen Participation: Poll, SNS (Facebook, Twitter), BBS, Single window link for online petition, Citizen proposal, Information Disclosure Request

In terms of citizen participation and interconnectedness, the MOGEF website is well-integrated with other national e-Government portals. For instance, the MOGEF website provides an embedded form that is connected to the central Government for Citizens (G4C), so that proposals and petitions pertaining to the work areas of MOGEF can be electronically filed and submitted either via the national G4C web portal or the MOGEF website.

Gender Objectives and Impact of Current e-Government Programmes
Overall, the result of Web Measurement Analysis in Republic of Korea indicates two interesting findings. First, the generally high score given to gender-related services and content, particularly regarding participation (64%), are possible due to the high level of overall e-Government presence in the country. Second, the MOGEF website has developed specialized services for women that can reach its constituencies even more effectively via online channels than traditional channels of delivery. For instance, online consulting services that run 24/7 on topics such as domestic violence and sexual harassment provide secure channels for women to seek expert opinions on discrete matters. Free cyber-mentoring and e-learning courses to improve women's entrepreneurship development and career building also contribute to achieving gender equality in public service delivery. In addition, through integrated platform, a mobile version of MOGEF website is being operated, through which users can received notifications and service updates via SMS or smartphone applications.

The Republic of Korea's experts who participated in the policy survey perceived e-government as an important vehicle of public service delivery for greater gender equality (64%), though they were not entirely satisfied with its contribution to inter-agency coordination and monitoring (42%). The respondents considered the provision of gender-equal access to government services as one of the most important goals of e-Government initiative (82%). The goal is also considered as being achieved effectively, as 75% of the respondents agreed or strongly agreed to its effectiveness. On the other hand, the respondents' view over the role of e-Government to ensure inter-agency monitoring and coordination, despite its perceived importance, was lower – only half of the respondents agreed with its effectiveness (42%, respectively). The result may reveal the participants' expectation to e-Government as a vehicle of greater gender advocacy, which goes beyond a mere service delivery mechanism within the boundary of the MOGEF.

Such a call for greater gender advocacy is also shown in the respondents' evaluation of the impact of e-Government to promote gender equality (72%). Though the survey participants generally valued its contribution, e-Government was considered as having made a relatively smaller contribution to promote political participation among women (38%).

Areas for Future Efforts
When asked to identify policy priorities, the respondents replied that it is critical to strengthen the monitoring role of e-Government as a data repository and watchtower of gender impacts of public services (72%) by monitoring gender impact of national programmes. Additionally,

respondents called for a thorough needs assessment to identify women's e-Government service needs and demands (68%). Most of the survey participants from Republic of Korea urged for a better assessment of women's e-Government service needs (68%). The result to a certain extent revealed that there is still a significant gap between the actual practice and the policy space, which should be filled with accurate understanding of situation and rigorous data collection.

Summary

Overall, experts from the Republic of Korea highly valued the MOGEF website, particularly in terms of its richness of information (72%), ease of access and use (68%), and effectiveness of online service transactions (68%). However, the levels of satisfaction were lower in areas concerning women's actual participation in the public sphere and its impact (42%) – again exhibiting a need for a greater emphasis on participation-oriented efforts for gender empowerment.

Box 9

Women Net Korea:
Integrated online service portal for Women

Women Net (www.women.go.kr) is an online public service portal for women operated by the Ministry of Gender Equality and Family of the Republic of Korea since its creation in 2002. The integrated online service portal, which stands alone from the national single window e-Government portal, can be considered as an alternative model to realize the potential of ICT application in gender administration and to broaden the scope and extent of online public services commonly considered within the national e-Government system.

Project Design

The inception of the Women Net came from the Basic Plan to Promote Women's Informatization (2002-2006), a national initiative pushed by the then-Ministry of Gender (MoG) of the Republic of Korea to improve women's ICT access and capacity. The Plan also included nurturing 1,000 women into ICT professionals in collaboration with women's tertiary education institutes. Under the slogan of "Digital MoG," the implementation of Women Net was carried out as a flagship project in 2002, with an aim to transform it into an online service hub for women through three project stages by 2006. In order to develop relevant service model and contents, MoG established an evaluation board comprising 300 experts from existing women networks, NGOs, vocational training institutes and tertiary education institutes.

Gender Empowerment

Online services are provided in 5 key areas, including the women crisis consulting, career coaching, family management, e-learning and web magazine.

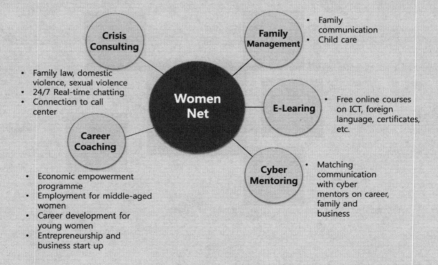

Career coaching and e-learning provides targeted education services that are tailored to the needs of different women groups in life stages for example new graduates from college and university, and women in their mid-ages re-entering the job market after a break due to marriage, childbirth or child caring. Online education programmes include resume coaching, guidebooks for successful employment, recruitment postings, career aptitude tests as well as key skills development courses on ICT, foreign languages and business management skills. Users can register at the homepage to receive free online coaching and access to online contents.

Diversified Delivery Channels

Cyber mentoring and counseling, the signature online services provided through the Women Net, realizes 24/7 access to emergency counseling on family law, domestic violence and sexual violence by adapting online chatting and mobile SMS. First, users can enter an open chatting window over the Internet where a certified duty counselor behind the line provides immediate guidance. Alternatively, users may reserve a session through the web system to receive a passcode via SMS text message which allows the user receive assistance either over the phone or through the chatting system.

Another noticeable feature of the Women Net is its integrated mobile platform through which users receive contents and consulting status updates via SMS text messages. Upon registration to the website, users may opt-in to its SMS notification service to be informed of any status changes to their coaching or consulting requests or new contents updates for their topics of interests through mobile phones. Users may send out free SMS messages through the Women Net websites depending on their activity and participation points.

Project Outcome

According the user statistics, the number of registered users of the site has showed a dramatic increase over the years, 42,000 in 2002 to almost 550,000 in 2011. The number of visitors also leaped from 420,000 in 2002 to almost 2,000,000. More than 80% of the registered users are women between their 20s and 40s, who tend to use free e-learning courses and career mentoring services, exhibiting their needs for career and skills development to increase social and economic participation. With the success of the initiative, MOGEF continues to develop targeted service models for Women Net, including the recently added content service on family management and child care.

3.1.10   Timor-Leste

The Secretary of State for the Promotion of
Equality (SSPE) is central in the Government of
Timor-Leste which is responsible for designing,
coordinating and executing the policy for the
areas of promotion and defense of gender equality.
It also supports the design of global and sector-
based policies to strengthen the role of Timorese
women in the society.

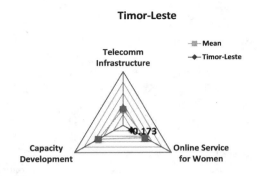

It is noticeable that very recently the SSPE
launched its official website after five years since
its creation in 2007. As the Secretary noted in the

**[Figure 19] Timor-Leste: e-Government
Readiness for Gender Equality**

website, the SSPE achieved a milestone in recognizing the growing needs to expand its outreach
and interaction with citizens. Overall, the website is at the Emerging stage, as it focuses on
disseminating key information on the SSPE, gender agendas, and documents and publications.
Some multimedia contents such as speeches and photos are available, though the extent of
resources provided through the website is still limited in terms of number of linked pages, due
partly to its short history of web presence.

As the country still goes through a transition period after the independence in 2002, it was not
possible to conduct a comparable analysis with other countries included in this research due to a
critical lack of globally available key statistics. However, the overall readiness in e-Government
online service appeared lower than the global average according to the latest EGDI in 2012, as
shown in the Framework Index.

[Table 17] Timor-Leste: SSPE Website Analysis

Secretary of State for the Promotion of Equality
Website: http://sepi.gov.tl
Language(s): Tetun, English
Online Service Level: Emerging
Interactions Available
  • G2C: Information dissemination for external users
  • G2E: Recruitments
Web Features
  • Information Dissemination: Organization Information, Links, News, Documents
  • Use & Accessibility: Search, Contacts, Multimedia, Multiple language
  • Service Delivery: N/A
  • Citizen Participation: N/A	

National Policies on ICT/ e-Government Development for Women

Participants replied that they are not aware of any ICT/e-Government policies specifically targeted for women (100%). Taking into account the relatively short history of its government in Timor-Leste after the conflict, the institutional structure in transition may have influenced such a result. Regarding the question of which agencies are currently exercising the greatest influence over policies concerning women's ICT and e-Government access, the participants exhibited a diverse range of answers that did not converge into any patterns, compared to other countries investigated in this research. However, the most number of respondents (60%) identified that the national ICT agency should take on the dominant role in future efforts.

Gender Objectives and Impact of Current e-Government Programmes

Respondents replied that building online communities for women (80%) and improving women's access to ICT (80%) are the two most important goals of e-Government initiatives aimed at gender equality. When requested to evaluate the current progress of the government, participants particularly appreciated that it supported women parliamentarians (60%), and contributed to promote women's political participation (60%). About the performance of the SSPE website, the majority of respondents did not agree that the website contributed in improving the degree of online service for women (60%). Again, considering the short history of online public services in e-Government, it is rather early to measure the progress, which was also mentioned in one of the comments made by the respondents.

Areas for Future Efforts

There were a wide range of responses made to the question to identify the challenges to gender inclusion in e-Government. More than a majority of respondents identified (55%) that it is important to conduct an adequate gender analysis of the ICT access, in order to solve the critical access divide prevalent in the country. In other suggestions, participants pointed out that the low level of contents and service relevance to the needs of women hinders women's adoption of e-Government services. Regarding the areas where further efforts are required, most participants identified the importance of developing institutional/staff capacity at the national gender machinery (60%) to design and carry out e-Government programmes.

Summary

In sum, the result of the policy survey revealed that currently, the experts did not consider the combination of e-Government and women as one of the priority areas of either ICT or gender administration. Considering the low level of telecommunication infrastructure readiness combined with a relatively low capability of public institutions and personnel in its public administration in transition, it is still early to evaluate the progress of gender inclusion in e-Government. The priority areas of focus should be to build an enabling environment in terms of infrastructure and capacity at the institutional level, while gradually raising awareness of stakeholders outside the government including women, NGOs and the private sector.[20]

---

[20] The response rate of experts in Timor-Leste was low, partly due to Timorese national election conducted during the survey period. Even though the number of survey responses received by the end of the survey period did not fulfill the threshold set for the country, analysis of Timor-Leste was included in the study in an effort to represent a small island, least developed country in the country groups.

3.1.11   Viet Nam

The National Committee for the Advancement of Women (NCAW) is an inter-ministerial body that advises the Prime Minister on gender equality and women's empowerment. The Minister of the Ministry of Labor, Invalids and Social Affairs (MOLISA) is designated as the president of NCAW, and the vice-chairs are the president of the Viet Nam Women's Union (VWU) and the Vice Minister of MOLISA.[21]

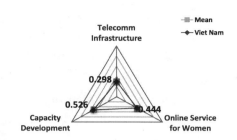

[Figure 20] Viet Nam: e-Government Readiness for Gender Equality

The web measurement analysis of the NCAW website revealed that the website provides an Emerging level online service to its citizens.[22] The website is composed of four main categories including the Introduction of the Committee, News and Events, Text and Publication Archives, and Contact Information. The Introduction of Committee section provides information on the vision, missions, organizational structure and contact directory of the committee as well as major laws and policies regarding gender empowerment. It has a separate news and events section where information about the latest events, publications and project updates are distributed in text and multimedia forms. Additionally, in the Text and Publication section, citizens can search the documents catalogue and download relevant data ranging from NCAW publications and legal documents to project performance reports from government agencies.

[Table 18] Viet Nam: NCAW Website Analysis

National Committee for the Advancement of Women
Website: http://hoilhpn.org.vn/
Language(s): Vietnamese
Online Service Level: Enhanced
Interactions Available
- G2C: Information dissemination for external users

Web Features
- Information Dissemination: Organization Information, Links, News, Documents
- Use & Accessibility: Search, Contacts, Multimedia
- Service Delivery: N.A
- Citizen Participation: Online petition

---

[21] Socialist Republic of Viet Nam, *Law on Domestic Violence Prevention and Control*, Law No. 02/2007/QH12, Hanoi, 2007.

[22] Since Viet Nam has multiple agencies at the central governmental level that address gender issues including MOLISA, NCAW and VWU, the research team consulted Vietnamese national experts and selected the NCAW and its website for the analysis of this research. Website: http://www.ubphunu-ncfaw.gov.vn

One notable issue about the web measurement analysis in Viet Nam is in regards to the interconnectedness of online services across different government authorities. As noted, multiple government entities including, but not limited to, the MOLISA, NCAW, and VWU, are involved in the design, development and implementation of the policies under the broader topic of gender equality in Viet Nam. However, they are not interconnected to ensure seamless transactions even though the three organizations mentioned have independent websites. For example, the MOLISA website provides a web link to NCAW as a specialized entity for gender equality but the NCAW website does not provide a link to MOLISA. Such fragmentation significantly limits the potential of a comprehensive online hub at the national level, as a single gateway to women-related information, services and participation.

The case of Viet Nam can provide further implications to countries where there are no single agency at the central government level that addresses the gender equality. Considering that the integrated e-Government services ultimately intend to provide a single window to access public services and a channel of participation, ensuring interconnectedness and integration among different websites is an important first step to strengthen online service delivery for women. It involves building an inter-agency framework to define roles and responsibilities, combining programme expertise and ICT skills, as well as agreeing upon a leadership and monitoring structure for the integrated online service hub for women.

Gender Objectives and Impact of Current e-Government Programmes
The result of the policy survey revealeld that respondents generally valued the impact of e-government to promote gender equality in public affairs. Most respondents agreed to the statement that the current government initiatives have contributed to deliver online social services for women (70%). However, the survey participants' answers showed a lower level of appreciation to its value as an input mechanism to enhance women's participation in decision-making process (44%).

Another notable finding is that even though the participants agreed to recognize the extended outreach of service delivery through the online means (82%), the perceived quality of those services did not match the same level of satisfaction (50%). It is an important distinction to note that the expansion of online service does not necessarily translate into the improvement of service quality.

This result may be understood in relation to the institutional and staff capacity that is responsible for the service development and implementation. As discussed earlier, the lack of inter-connectedness among different websites that are operated by multiple divisions of government may indicate a weak inter-agency structure for gender-related online service provision. When a coherent service framework is not present, it is more likely to have duplicate contents or a grey area that reduces the overall quality of services.

Areas for Future Efforts

Concerns over the quality of service are also reflected in the respondents' answers to the policy priorities. Most participants (30%) identified that developing institutional and staff capacity is one of the most urgent tasks to improve e-Government for women, emphasizing the inter-agency coordination and capacity building of the government to ensure coherent, seamless online services for women. Another 25% of the respondents answered that it is critical to understand women's e-government service needs, which warrants the distinction between the quantity and quality aspects of e-Government for women.

Summary

In sum, the result of the Vietnamese policy survey revealed that the respondents agreed that the primary value of e-Government lies in providing better access to information and public services for gender equality, and the policy priorities should be set on identifying women's online service needs and strengthening institutional capacity.

3.2 Key Findings of the Analysis

This section provides an analysis of the data collected about the perceived effectiveness of e-Government to promote gender equality. Before presenting the results, it is important to note that analyzing significant patterns within these survey results does not mean that the findings can be generalized on a cross-country level. Conversely, the aim of this summary lies in providing a point for further research about the implications of e-Government provision for women's empowerment that originate within the specific initiatives of the national machinery of gender equality while acknowledging the different cultural contexts.

3.2.1   Defining the Scope of e-Government Objectives for Gender Inclusion

E-Government is a relatively new concept in public administration and the scope and extent of its definition have evolved significantly as technology and the level of awareness of stakeholders have ripened. Gender equality in this still changing concept of e-Government inevitably embraces the same essential task, as to how to define the scope of its key objectives and goals. Naturally, the formulation of such a shared vision of gender equality in e-Government should vary from country to country, depending on the level of ICT and e-Government, gender development, and other socioeconomic factors. This section mainly presents snapshots of the ***perceived scope of e-Government initiatives*** for gender equality in terms of their goals and progress.

To the question concerning how to define the key objectives of e-Government for greater gender equality, the respondents drew attention to a broad range of policy issues, from prerequisites such as ICT access and capacity to concerns of improving outreach and participation. The status of e-Government and gender equality programmes across the featured countries may account for the different perceptions of the respondents regarding priority policies for future e-Government initiatives in their countries.

[Figure 21] Scope of e-Government Objectives for Gender Equality

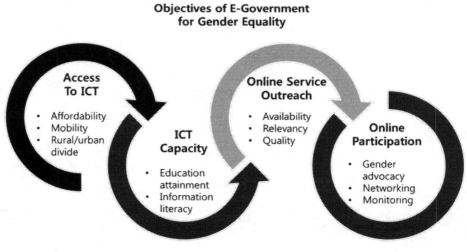

70

As shown in the figure above, the answers could be categorized into four core areas including women's access to ICT, their ICT capacity, public service outreach for women and their participation into society through online channel. In those four areas at the intersection of women, ICT and public administration interests, it was the specific situation of a country's gender development, ICT advancement, as well as e-Government service capacity which jointly influenced the respondents' perceived scope of objectives for gender equality in e-Government.

Box 10

Measuring the Gender Digital Divide:
Access and Capacity

In order to adequately address the gender digital divide, it is important to understand different dimensions of the divide and develop measurement index to highlight the gap.

As noted, the digital divide goes beyond the simple access gap; it includes the capacity to use the information and communication tools as well as the quality of utilization that contributes to sustainable development, i.e. the use of ICT for productive or educational purposes. The figure below, adapted from the *Explanation Frame of the Digital Divide* by Szilárd Molnár illustrates three different dimensions of the digital divide.

Number of Users

Adoption Stage	Early Adoption	Take-off	Saturation
Types	Access divide	Usage divide	Divide stemming from the quality of use
Terms	Early digital divide	Primary Digital divide (Quantity of use)	Secondary Digital divide (Quality of use)
Description	Divide between those with access and without access	Divide between users and non-users	Divide between users
S-curve of ICT Diffusion			

The suggested gender digital divide index should consider the following as its key objectives.

- Provide policy indicators displaying gender gap in information access, capacity, and use
- Assess degree of gender digital divide and draw out key characteristics of women's ICT usage and needs pattern
- Contribute to bridging gender gap in e-Government access and utilization
- Provide baseline information for policy and programme development in e-Government
- Serve as performance indicators for project outcomes

Notably, as shown in the figure below, respondents from the countries that comprise the emerging level of e-Government replied that improving women's ICT access and capacities are the most critical objective, whereas they identified gender advocacy for improved outreach and participation as less important. On the other hand, the countries in the connected stage, in particular Republic of Korea, placed more importance on gender advocacy and monitoring, and displayed a significantly different pattern from the rest of the countries.

[Figure 22] Objectives of e-Government by development stage

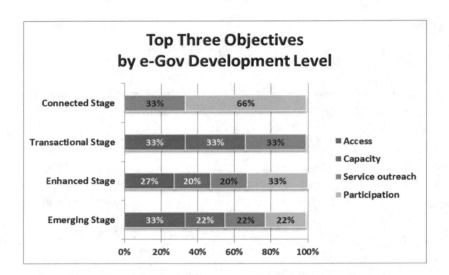

In particular, the respondents' comment revealed the following as major concerns in regards to improving e-government: the institutional and human capacity of the Ministry: the question of how to 'add value' to existing programmes by applying ICT; finding the right balance between 'gender policy focus' and knowledge of ICT operations; improving the integration of national e-Government policy and Ministry initiatives; increasing clarity between the respective roles of the ICT department and policy development/implementation department; improving the measurement of e-Government performance; improving communication with stakeholders including women's networks and other government agencies; identifying women's ICT and online service needs; and building a demand base of e-Government services for women.

The respondents identified a variety of obstacles to promoting gender equality in e-Government in their countries. As shown in the following table, access and capacity divides (rural and urban divide, income inequality) were relevant to Bangladesh, People's Republic of China, Fiji, Malaysia, Mongolia, the Philippines, and Timor-Leste. Content and service relevance was considered important in People's Republic of China, and, India, Indonesia, Malaysia, and Mongolia. Respondents from Bangladesh, Republic of Korea, and Viet Nam mentioned that it is very critical to understand sociocultural aspects such as women's attitudes and usage patterns of ICT.

[Table 19] Major Obstacles by Areas

Areas	Major Obstacles	Countries
ICT Access	Lack of affordable access for women	Bangladesh, Indonesia, Malaysia, The Philippines
	Lack of gender analysis in the telecommunication industry	People's Republic of China, Fiji, Mongolia, Timor-Leste
Capacity	Different gender patterns of technology use	Bangladesh, Republic of Korea, The Philippines
	Attitudes of women towards technology	People's Republic of China, Viet Nam
	Language barrier	Timor-Leste
Service Outreach	Lack of national data/statistics on women's ICT usage	People's Republic of China, Fiji, India
	Lack of contents and information relevant women's needs	India, Indonesia, Republic of Korea, Malaysia, Viet Nam
	Lack of inter-agency coordination across the government	Fiji, Mongolia, Viet Nam
	Inadequate government staff's expertise in ICT	India, Timor-Leste
Participation & Advocacy	Lack of gender friendly framework in public administration	Fiji, India, Republic of Korea, Mongolia, The Philippines

3.2.2 Online Service Delivery for Women

E-Government directly impacts sustainable development through the use of ICT in the social and economic development programmes of the public sector (UNDESA, 2012). In this sense, e-Government may lead to the opportunities offered by ICT to promote gender empowerment, with online services specifically targeted to the socioeconomic needs of women. The topic has a ramification on to how policy makers define *the extent of online services* for women under the e-Government framework.

This section provides a trend of online service delivery for women that is identified from the 11 selected countries according to four different subtopics, which are: documents and information on laws and policies; technical features (audio, video, RSS, SNS, etc.) as a conduit of information and service flow; areas of public services for women; and features for online based participation.

A review of the online presence of national gender machineries from the 11 countries indicates that countries put efforts into providing relevant and up-to-date information and services for women. All of the investigated countries offered information that was updated within a month, and provided a site map or index to help users navigate through its online contents and services.

73

[Figure 23] Online features available through national gender websites

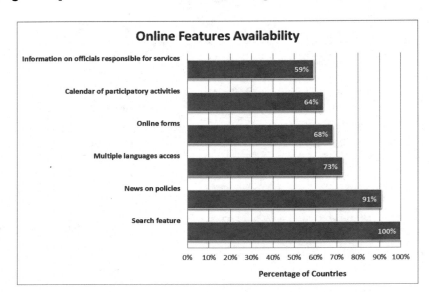

Available services and features for women showed a spectrum in terms of their extent and variety depending on the level of overall e-Government development of each country. The most common and basic features were documentations of laws and policies pertaining to gender empowerment. Except for Bangladesh, Fiji, Mongolia and Timor-Leste, all other countries provided options for directly sending updates via email, RSS or a mobile device to users. Except for Bangladesh, Fiji, and the Philippines, all others offered multiple language access to their national gender websites.

In terms of the thematic areas of service for women, most countries offered services in education and health. However, the degree of service varied significantly from one country to another, as only a few offered features with transactional capability, such as online talent registration (Republic of Korea), financial application (Malaysia), and online petition (India).

[Figure 24] Online Service by Areas

Online Services by Areas

Petition/Consulting: Online Forms 7, Downloadable Forms 1, Archived Information 5
Labour: Online Forms 1, Downloadable Forms 6, Archived Information 7
Social Welfare: Online Forms 2, Downloadable Forms 5, Archived Information 11
Health: Online Forms 1, Downloadable Forms 4, Archived Information 4
Education: Online Forms 2, Downloadable Forms 3, Archived Information 3
Laws and Policies: Online Forms 0, Downloadable Forms 2, Archived Information 11

Legend:
- Online Forms
- Downloadable Forms
- Archived Information

X-axis: Number of Countries (0 to 12)

Most of the 11 countries have some means of collecting user opinion online; however, there was a difference among countries in terms of their technical sophistication and variety ranging from online polls and text-based feedback forms to real-time chat rooms. Such e-Consultation tools (UNDESA, 2012) available at the national gender website includes simple online feedback forms, online polls, email groups, and SNS.

[Figure 25] Usage of participation tools at national gender websites

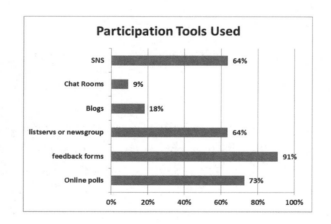

Participation Tools Used

- SNS: 64%
- Chat Rooms: 9%
- Blogs: 18%
- listservs or newsgroup: 64%
- feedback forms: 91%
- Online polls: 73%

X-axis: 0% to 100%

Particularly, the use of SNS, such as Facebook and Twitter, is identified in the majority of countries surveyed, except for Bangladesh, Fiji, Timor-Leste and Viet Nam. By using the existing users already active in SNS, more people are able to access up-to-date information on important gender policies and programmes, as well as participate in online polls and leave comments and suggestions.[23]

---

[23] See Box 8 for the case of SNS application in the Philippines

75

The service levels of the surveyed countries strongly correlate with the country's level of telecommunication infrastructure development compared to other factors considered in this research[24], indicating the importance of surmounting the digital divide as a pre-requisite to achieving a greater impact of e-Government for gender empowerment. However, the lack of internationally comparable data to gauge the gender digital divide hinders further analysis in this regard, as it is not possible to filter out the pure impact of the ICT access barrier to women.

[Figure 26] Online Service for Women by Telecom Infrastructure

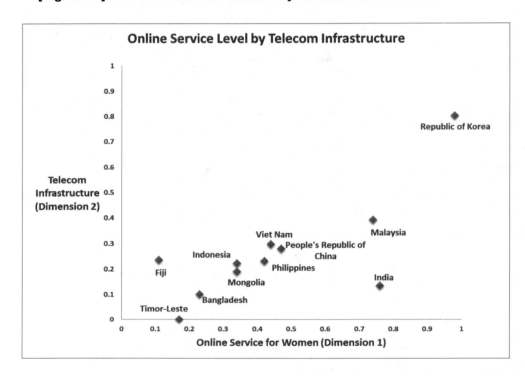

In conclusion, countries in their emerging and enhanced stages of development need to continue to focus on expanding the scope and variety of online services for women, as well as consolidating services and information to improve the user convenience and ease. In addition, an increasing emphasis must be put on the assessment of the level of service usage and user satisfaction, as to how online services are effectively meeting the demands of women, and more fundamentally, to ensure whether the e-Government environment is conducive in creating such a demand from women, a vulnerable group in society that faces the digital divide in terms of access to ICT infrastructure and capacity. In this regard, further research in policy areas should focus on gauging input from the demand side of the e-Government initiatives for gender equality.

---

[24] Except for Fiji and India.

3.2.3 Integration and Coordination

Increasingly, e-Government in many countries evolves into a single-window model, which emphasizes a seamless integration of information and services that have been traditionally provided in different government departments and agencies. Considering that the disadvantages women face encompass political, economic, social and cultural concerns and are complexly ingrained in society, the public service provision through e-government poses an advantage arising from the integrated approach. Here lies the potential of e-Government to mainstream the gender equality in the entire realm of public administration, rather than having it remain as an isolated island under the national gender machinery.

Based on the online survey that was conducted in 11 countries, this section presents a snapshot of country experts' perception on how the e-Government for gender equality addresses the call for collaborative responses from different actors within government and within the society as a whole. Topics include the way in which online public services for women are coordinated and implemented across the government, and the potential of e-Government to re-engineer the process of existing gender policy development and transform the gender governance in the long run.

> **Box 11**
>
> **Engaging with Women NGOs e-AWEDAN, India**
>
> e-AWEDAN (Electronic Application for Women Empowerment and Development Action by NGOs) is an online platform developed by the Central Social Welfare Board (CSWB) of India with an aim to engage in and empower women NGOs through the online space. Building an online community of existing women's network is an important task in gender inclusion initiatives for e-Government; it not only serves as an effective needs base for women-centric online services but offers expertise and key contents proven on the ground. By streamlining the data transfer between the MWCD, the funding agency, and CSWB regional boards in 33 states, and applicant NGOs, the platform aims to strengthen the online presence of women NGOs and to improve programme effectiveness and transparency.
>
> http://eawedan.gov.in

The result revealed that the gap is not yet bridged between the two realms of gender development and e-Government. An examination of suggestions made by experts to improve the online service of the national gender website revealed that the most frequently used words by respondents with ICT backgrounds were usability, interconnectedness and transaction, whereas these words never appeared in the suggestions from those with a gender development background. Conversely, experts from the gender domain tend to emphasize ICT training, education and staff capacity as key recommendations.

In most of the surveyed countries (64%), respondents emphasized the importance of institutional framework across the government as a necessary precondition to pursue gender inclusion in e-Government. Toward the question of whether the country has an apex organization of gender and ICT, which provides coordination among different government departments, survey participants from most countries replied negatively (64%). The result also relates to the absence of a national ICT policy and strategy in most of the countries, which should define the country's vision of gender inclusion in e-Government and spell out the designated leading agency and supporting organizations within the government system, as well as their respective roles and responsibilities. As shown in the figure below, the G2G level interactions through the national gender websites displayed the lowest progress compared to other levels of communication.

[Figure 27] e-Government Interactions via national gender websites

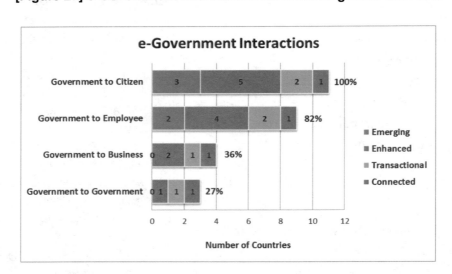

With regard to how gender initiatives for e-Government are planned and implemented, respondents from most countries identified the lack of coordination between the national gender machinery and the Ministry of ICT or equivalent as a problem (54%). To the question of which actor currently has the strongest influence and ownership over polices relating to gender inclusion in e-Government, most of the respondents identified the Ministry of ICT or equivalent (36%), which was closely followed by the national gender machinery or equivalent (33%) and the central government agency such as the President/Prime Minister's Office (27%). On the other hand, when asked which should play a leading role, there were more respondents that emphasized that the Ministry of ICT or equivalent should take responsibility in fully incorporating gender inclusion into its list of priorities (42%).

The result to a certain degree reflects the perception of the country respondents that gender initiatives have not been fully incorporated in the national ICT and e-Government policies, with the risks of isolation and low sustainability. Notwithstanding the important input the national gender machinery has to provide in the domain knowledge expertise of gender equality, many respondents suggested that gender mainstreaming take place in e-Government, which is ultimately led by the apex organization in national ICT and e-Government development. In particular, participants mentioned that the policy conversation and shared learning between the two departments should be encouraged as a starting point of cross-government coordination, in order to prevent further horizontal fragmentation. In some countries including India, the lack of vertical coordination was also identified as a major problem; the national initiatives and visions are difficult to be shared down to the local government.

When suggested to address such lack of coordination and fragmentation, many respondents emphasized the importance of a strong commitment at the top-level and the political 'push' it allows. More specifically, a priority should be placed on setting up a shared vision for gender inclusion in e-Government, which should be closely aligned with the national e-Government development plans. With specific vision statements and political leaders who share them, it is easier to draw out the institutional framework and allocate financial and human resources, and thereby to move on to the next stage of setting up strategies, specific targets of implementation and monitoring. The establishment of national gender Informatization plan in Republic of Korea can be considered as an example of this commitment. In addition, experts suggested the importance of human capacity in national gender machinery.

Along with the shared vision and coordination framework notably between the national gender machinery and across the government, it is important to ensure the seamless flow of information and the integration and interoperability of services and systems deployed. For example, the online petition systems for gender-related violence in India can be further integrated with systems in relevant policing or judiciary agencies to facilitate the process.

> **Box 12**
>
> **Gender Statistics Information System (GSIS), Republic of Korea**
>
> Gender disaggregated statistics are a key piece of information to improve the efficacy and relevancy of online public service programmes for women. The Korean Women's Development Institute (KWDI), a leading public think tank for gender policy in Republic of Korea has established an information portal where gender-disaggregated statistics from central and local level government agencies as well as international sources including such as MDG statistics can be accessed through a single window. Additionally, the KWDI researchers on a regular basis reproduce existing statistics into *themed statistics*, which utilize graphical tools and online campaigns in an effort to expand the audience base for the gender-disaggregated statistics.
>
> With this, the GSIS information portal serves two goals: first, to meet the gender-data needs from the local governments where information resources and gender-sensitive policy expertise are relatively scarce and; second, to raise awareness of the public in general.
>
> http://gsis.kwdi.re.kr/gsis/eg/main.html

One of the key factors to assess the system integration in e-Government is the degree of incorporation with a single national window. While not all countries provide a single national window for e-Government yet, some countries provide a gateway to their national page or portal by linking them to the website of their national gender machinery, notably including People's Republic of China, India, Republic of Korea, Malaysia, Mongolia, and Timor-Leste.

However, the link to a national portal does not necessarily imply the interoperability of data, interface and backend operation. Initiatives for greater gender inclusion in e-Government should cover beyond the integration of different technologies and systems used, and consider the possibility of realizing an integrated, systematic assistance for a more harmonized online service for women.

To make such a women-centric design and delivery of online services realized across the national e-Government framework, it is of foremost importance to set up an integrated database of women's needs, access and usage of ICT and e-Government. A systematic collection and management of gender-disaggregated ICT data paves ways to an evidence-based policy development, which can be easily shared, implemented and monitored. The survey result of 11 countries reflects this finding. Respondents recognized the importance of gender-disaggregated ICT database in assessing women's service needs for e-Government and monitoring the gender impact of national e-Government plans. In countries such as Fiji, Indonesia, and Viet Nam, respondents highlighted the fact that such information is not collected at the national level and urged to develop an initiative through a standalone pilot project under the national gender machinery or by implementing a policy toolkit produced as a regional or international cooperation programme.

In sum, it is highly important to set up an institutional coordination framework and garner necessary political support by engaging top-level leaders. The sustainability and efficacy of initiatives can be secured with the internal motive and energy, required resources and concrete implementation structure.

4. Toolkit: e-Government for Gender Equality Action Plan

The Readiness Framework assessment highlights the strengths and weaknesses of a country on different aspects of e-Government for gender equality, in terms of its infrastructure, gender development and e-Government technical sophistication. It helps the government identify which sectors are more prepared to embrace gender equality initiatives in the e-Governance, and which community or stakeholders are more prepared to contribute to and benefit from the e-Government initiatives. This in turn sheds light on identifying the priority areas of e-Government and critical areas for further investment in improving gender impact in the public administration as a whole.

Once the readiness assessment has been conducted and ground realities about the state of preparedness of a country are known, an achievable strategy has to be crafted that will not only help in an effective implementation of e-Government initiatives for gender equality, but also integrate the gender principle across the government.

Although there are no standard guidelines or processes available for devising e-Government action plans for greater gender equality, which could be uniformly applied to all countries, this chapter presents a set of suggested steps to formulate a national action plan. Based on the results of the policy survey and the framework analysis of eleven countries, the following section provides a toolkit to develop an action plan, with an aim to touch upon all stages of e-Government development from developing a national vision for gender equality in e-Government to establishing requisite infrastructure, and from formulation of laws to setting baseline database and performance benchmarks. The broad design of the toolkit steps were in part adopted from UNESCO's *E-Government Toolkit for Developing Countries* (UNESCO, 2005).

4.0   Understand Readiness: Country Grouping

Before following the general guidelines for action plan, it is important to understand where the policy priority should be placed among the myriads of tasks entailed in the process. Even though specific strengths and weaknesses may vary from country to country, a categorization of countries according to key characteristics regarding gender and e-Government would help countries identify priorities and seek targeted recommendations.

Here, based on the Analysis Framework discussed in Chapter 3, country grouping was conducted in a 2 by 2 matrix as below, taking the degree of **e-Government online service capacity** along the x axis and **gender gap in online service provision** along the y axis as defining factors.

[Figure 28] Gender Gap in Online Service Capacity

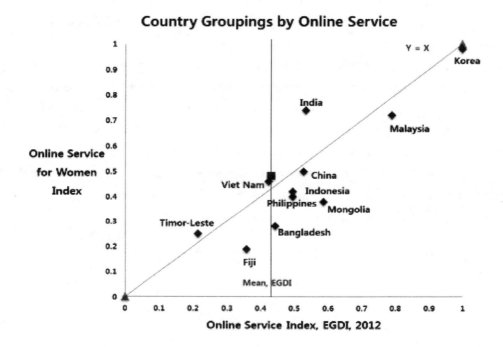

[Figure 29] Country Grouping by Online Service Capacity

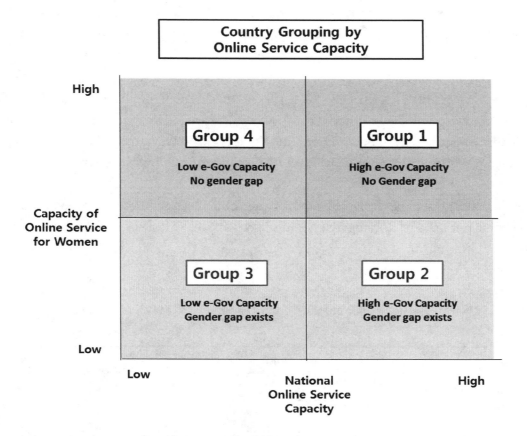

Group 1 represents countries that have already achieved a level of national e-Government service capacity above the global average. Their online services for women do not exhibit a gender gap compared to other areas of online public services, for example, health, finance, education, etc. It is more likely that these countries have a national strategy already set in place for gender inclusion in e-Government. Policy priorities for countries in this category should be placed as having a greater gender *advocacy* that effectively connects online and offline activities, so that e-Government can serve as a transformative means to change the gender inequality in society as a whole.

Countries in Group 2 exhibit advanced capacity in e-Government service, but their technical and administrative know-hows have not yet been fully embodied in the gender governance. Many recent follower countries in e-Government tend to fall under this category. In this sense, policy makers should consider expanding the gender service outreach, particularly through *raising awareness* of the potential benefit of targeted online service provision for women, and building a functioning *institutional framework* across government departments and external partners to embark on mutual collaboration.

Countries in group 3 have a below-average level of capacity in e-Government service, and it is likely that the countries show generally low level of ICT infrastructure development, which is a prerequisite to equitable access to online services. In many cases, consequently, gender programmes in e-Government initiatives are not actively pursued as the Internet has not been rooted as an affordable channel of communication. Countries in this category should pursue policies focused *on infrastructure development* and the provision of equitable technology access for women, and the development of human capacity within the government as well as the public in general.

Group 4 represents countries that have relatively outperforming online services in gender administration compared to the relatively low level of national e-Government capacity. Policy priorities in this category may include improving the general e-Government capacity through awareness raising and setting up of *national vision* for e-Government development.

The table below illustrates the topics covered in the following toolkit and suggested areas of priority according to the country categorization discussed above. This prioritization aims to direct the attention of decision makers from a particular group to the modules that might be most relevant to their current level of readiness.

[Table 20] Toolkit Topics

Topic	Activities	Target Groups
4.1. Define national vision	Define vision statement Develop strategic goals	Groups 2,4
4.2. Raise awareness	Secure top-level commitment	Groups 2,3
	Communicate with women	Groups 1,2
4.3. Establish a focal organization	Designate a focal organization	Groups 2,3
	Develop an institutional framework	Groups 2,3,4
	Conduct research and training	Groups 2,3
4.4. Establish a gender database	Collect women's demand information	Groups 1,2,3,4
	Monitor gender impact of e-Government	Groups 1,4
4.5. Build human capacity	Build women's ICT capacity	Group 3
	Build institutional capacity	Groups 2,3
4.6. Ensure technology access	Ensure connectivity with existing resources	Groups 3,4
	Consider m-Government	Groups 2,3,4
4.7. Define laws and policies	Safeguard women from cybercrimes	Groups 1,2,3,4
	Ensure system integration	Groups 2,4
4.8. Establish partnerships	Collaborate with NGOs	Groups 1,2,3
	Set up research institutes	Groups 2,4
	Partner with international organizations	Groups 3,4
4.9. Conduct pilot projects	Identify a pilot area	Groups 2,3
	Implement pilot project	Groups 2,3
	Scale up	Groups 2,4

[Figure 30] Suggested Combination of Policy Priorities by Groups

Group 1: Advocacy Priority

Focus Areas	Key Related Steps Action Plan
Access	4.1. Define national vision
	4.6. Ensure technology access
	4.7. Define laws and policies*
Capacity	4.2. Raise awareness*
	4.5. Build human capacity
	4.8. Establish partnerships*
Service Outreach	4.3. Establish a focal organization
	4.4. Establish a gender database
	4.7. Define laws and policies*
	4.9. Conduct pilot projects
Advocacy	4.2. Raise awareness*
	4.8. Establish partnerships*
	4.9. Conduct pilot projects*

Group 2: Service Outreach Priority

Focus Areas	Key Related Steps Action Plan
Access	4.1. Define national vision
	4.6. Ensure technology access
	4.7. Define laws and policies*
Capacity	4.2. Raise awareness*
	4.5. Build human capacity
	4.8. Establish partnerships*
Service Outreach	4.3. Establish a focal organization
	4.4. Establish a gender database
	4.7. Define laws and policies*
	4.9. Conduct pilot projects
Advocacy	4.2. Raise awareness*
	4.8. Establish partnerships*
	4.9. Conduct pilot projects*

Group 3: Access Priority

Focus Areas	Key Related Steps Action Plan
Access	4.1. Define national vision
	4.6. Ensure technology access
	4.7. Define laws and policies*
Capacity	4.2. Raise awareness*
	4.5. Build human capacity
	4.8. Establish partnerships*
Service Outreach	4.3. Establish a focal organization
	4.4. Establish a gender database
	4.7. Define laws and policies*
	4.9. Conduct pilot projects
Advocacy	4.2. Raise awareness*
	4.8. Establish partnerships*
	4.9. Conduct pilot projects*

Group 4: Capacity Priority

Focus Areas	Key Related Steps Action Plan
Access	4.1. Define national vision
	4.6. Ensure technology access
	4.7. Define laws and policies*
Capacity	4.2. Raise awareness*
	4.5. Build human capacity
	4.8. Establish partnerships*
Service Outreach	4.3. Establish a focal organization
	4.4. Establish a gender database
	4.7. Define laws and policies*
	4.9. Conduct pilot projects
Advocacy	4.2. Raise awareness*
	4.8. Establish partnerships*
	4.9. Conduct pilot projects*

4.1   Define a National Vision for Gender Inclusion in e-Government

At the first stage of the e-Government initiative for a greater gender equality, it is important to set up a national vision for the purpose of considering the unique situations of its priorities and resources.

Vision Statement

A vision statement should define what it means to promote greater gender equality in the e-Government initiative and what aims it should achieve through this measure. The vision statement should focus on the primary stakeholder and beneficiary, women, and relevant stakeholders including women, government, NGOs and others should be involved so as to ensure their participation and adoption. The statement should also be aligned with the existing national e-Government vision if the government has already set one up.

Strategic Goals

The vision statement should also be accompanied by a list of priority areas for the implementation of e-Government programmes, based on key sectors in the economy of the country as well as its readiness. Strategic goals will have to be derived from the vision statement, which should set the tone for building up an action framework.

[Figure 31] Vision Statement and Strategic Goals

Additional resource links for this step

Category	Resource Type	Title	Organization	Index Number[25]
Vision Statement	Primer	Gender Responsive E-governance: Exploring the Transformative Potential	United Nations Development Programme (UNDP)	01
	Checklist	Checklist for the Planning Design and Implementation of an ICT Project Incorporating Gender Issues	The World Bank	02
	Policy Report	Gender and ICT	United Nations Development Programme – Asia-Pacific Development Information Programme (UNDP-APDIP)	03

---

[25] Annex A provides further descriptions of the resources.

4.2   Raise Awareness

After establishing a vision, it is vital to communicate the gender equality principle with key stakeholders. Priority should be placed on formulating two-tier communication strategy, one targeting the top-level political leadership and the other aiming the broader public.

Political Leadership

Exposure to the top-level leadership of the country can make much difference as their awareness on the gender equality topic in e-Government can give the initiative the necessary political will. The top-level leadership may include the head of the State, Prime Minister, Ministers of government departments and other senior executives. This awareness can be generated through various means, from demonstrating the examples and case studies of gender equality in e-Government from other countries to attending seminars or high-level meetings on the topic typically organized at regional or international levels.

[Figure 32] Proposed e-Gov Awareness Workshop Modules for Public Officials

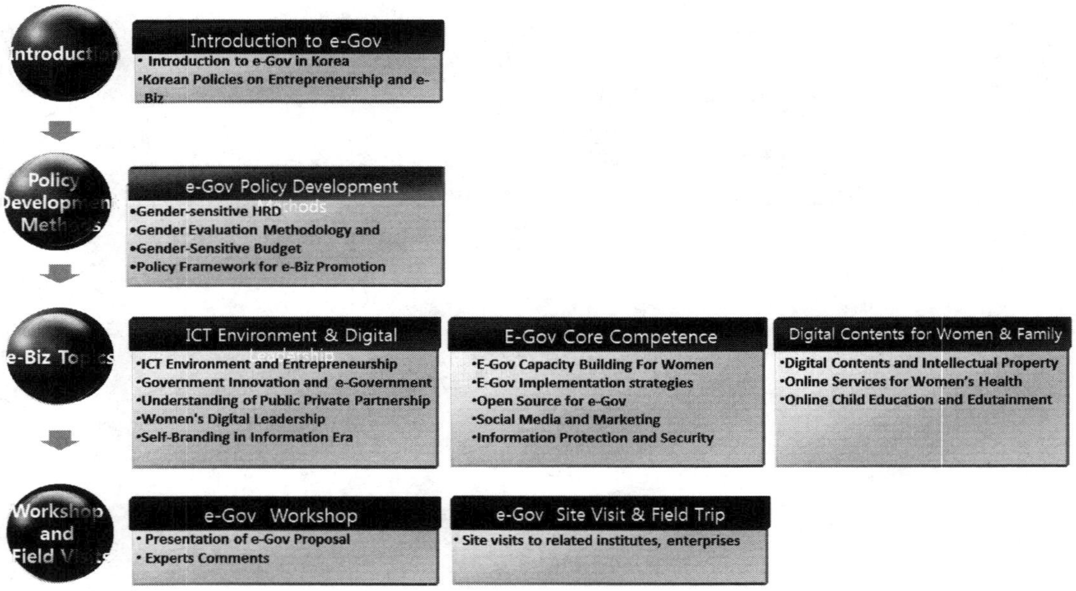

Citizen Awareness Communication Strategy

Once the commitment from the political leadership and senior-level officials are sufficient, the strategies to raise the awareness of the broader public, particularly including women, should kick in. Specialized promotion and advertising programmes can be considered to spread the awareness about the benefits and imperatives of greater gender equality in e-Government, along with relevant education and outreach programmes. This step may consider utilizing SNS for public outreach.

Additional resource links for this step

Category	Resource Type	Title	Publisher	Index Number
Awareness Raising	Policy report	ICT and gender equality: new opportunities and challenges for public administration to implement the internationally agreed development goals, including the Millennium Development Goals	United Nations Economic and Social Council (UNECOSOC)	04
	Toolkit	Engendering ICT Toolkit: Challenges and Opportunities for Gender-Equitable Development	World Bank	05
	Policy report	Information and communication technologies and their impact on and use as an instrument for the advancement and empowerment of women	UNDAW/DESA	06

4.3   Establish a Focal Organization

For a vision of gender equality in e-Government to become a reality at the national level, it is important to have an apex organization or institution in the government system to initiate, implement and monitor the effective implementation.

Role of Focal Organization

Key roles of the **focal organization** should include, among others, the following.

- Serve as a primary architect of online-based public services targeted for women's needs
- Design and develop targets, standards, policies and guidelines related to gender inclusion in e-Government
- Provide consultancy inputs to individual e-Government projects on gender inclusion issues
- Play the role of an anchor in gender monitoring of various e-Government initiatives to ensure the system's interconnectedness

In many countries, candidates that are eligible to take on the role of focal organizations can be summarized into two major categories, first, the existing central authority for e-Government, and second, the national gender machinery.

Inter-agency Coordination Model

In case the e-Government / ICT agency takes the leading role, it is more advantageous to ensure the system integration and policy coordination across the e-Government system. On the other hand, a gender-focused model allows domain expertise in gender equality to be applied to the service development and delivery, potentially deriving a greater programme relevancy and usefulness for the beneficiary.

- There should be a horizontal approach, according to which governmental gender equality organizations take the initiative to provide initial information services for women, and subsequently seek to establish networks with national e-Government integration
- Simultaneously, there should be a top-down approach, where the agency responsible for national e-Government initiatives provides programmes relevant for marginalized citizens, including women as a major subgroup

These two approaches are not mutually exclusive and can be used in combinations according to the situation faced by each country.

[Figure 33] Gender Priority Model   **[Figure 34] e-Gov Priority Model**

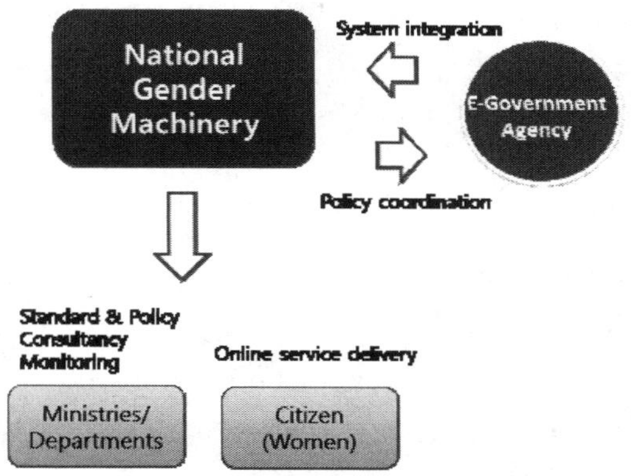

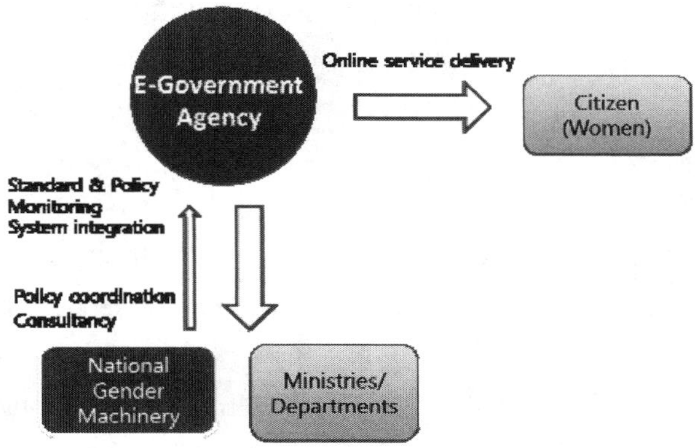

Even though the conditions each country face may influence its choice between the two models of focal organization, it is critical to establish **a model of inter-agency coordination for gender inclusion** and thus identify an entity across the government agencies to serve as a focal point for e-Government provision for women. During the process, it is important to define the roles and responsibilities between the national gender machinery and the government agencies responsible for national e-Government initiatives, so that online services for women are not isolated within the realm of gender development, but to be fully interconnected with other national e-Government initiatives.

In addition, the focal organization should consider setting up a research and training division under which focused research projects can be carried out to localize appropriate implementation and participatory solutions to meet women's online service needs. Furthermore, trainings can be conducted to build up the institutional capacity of technical and gender programme aspects of e-Government.

Additional resource links for this step

Category	Resource Type	Title	Publisher	Index Number
Establish a focal organization	Policy report	Researching ICT-Based Enterprise for Women in Developing Countries: A Gender Perspective	Institute for Development Policy and Management (IDPM)	07
	Evaluation report	Evaluation of Gender Mainstreaming in UNDP	UNDP	08

4.4   Establish a Gender Database

When developing specific gender programmes for e-Government, it may span a number of activities, from gathering baseline data to gauge programme demand to collecting feedback on service and content supply, and monitoring the programme implementation and impact.

Demand Side Information: Women's ICT Needs

First, on the demand side, it is critical to map the current status of women's ICT access and e-Government use, as well as potential service needs through extensive data collection. The outreach aspect should always be based on the analysis of key characteristics of women and their areas of information needs. In this sense, **gender-disaggregated data collection** of different dimensions of ICT environments is critical to adequately understand the current gender gap and use the findings to create policies for improved relevancy and impact. Such activity requires close coordination with other relevant agencies, including the national machinery of ICT / e-Government and the national statistics office.

In addition to the gendered-ICT data collection at the individual level, it is also important to collect and understand the needs of women's development NGOs and grassroots networks, as well as women-owned businesses. Targeted need assessment of these established groups and businesses will strengthen the presence of gender networks in online spaces and subsequently support the development and dissemination of relevant services for women through collective need and intelligence.

[Table 21] Suggested Areas of Gender-disaggregated Statistics Collection

Areas	Factors	Key gender-disaggregated statistics
Access	Access to ICT Ownership of ICT devices Capacity of ICT devices	Access to public access points (telecentres, etc.) Ownership of PC, mobile devices Time takes to access PC when needed Time takes to access internet when needed Types of ICT devices most frequently used Types of internet access most frequently used
Capacity	Computer usage capacity Internet usage capacity	OS and utility programmes, multimedia, computer graphics, word processing programmes, etc. Web browser, information search, online multimedia, email, e-Government and other online transactions, etc.
Use	Quantitative usage Qualitative usage	PC usage rate, internet usage rate, daily PC and internet usage time Perceived usefulness of PC and internet usage in areas including: work/business, education, leisure, social activities, e-Government, etc. Degree of usage of PC and internet for recommended areas including: information search, document creation and management, online transactions, online education, participation to society, and community activities, etc.

Box 13

Unveiling the Online Gender Gap: "Women and the Web" Report by Intel

Intel Corporation released a groundbreaking report on "Women and the Web," in January 2013, unveiling concrete data on the enormous Internet gender gap in the developing world and the social and economic benefits of securing Internet access for women. To better understand the gender gap, Intel commissioned this study and consulted with the UN Women, U.S. State Department's Office of Global Women's Issues, and World Pulse, a global network for women.

As the first comprehensive study on how women and girls use the Internet, it reports that the gender gap in women's access to the Internet is even greater than that of mobile phones, with women being 23 percent less likely to use the Internet in low-to-medium income countries. That gap soars to 43 percent in sub-Saharan Africa, where men are almost twice as likely to have access to the Internet as women. This lack of access is giving rise to a second digital divide, one where women and girls risk being left further and further behind. The report issues a call to action to double the number of women online from 600 million as of 2012 to 1.2 billion in the next three years, both by bridging the gender gap and broadening overall access in developing countries.

The report's findings are based on interviews and surveys of 2,200 women and girls living in urban and peri-urban areas of four focus countries: Egypt, India, Mexico and Uganda, as well as analyses of global databases.

Source:
Intel Announces Groundbreaking 'Women and the Web' Report with UN Women and State Department, Intel Newsroom, Intel Homepage, 2013.
http://newsroom.intel.com/community/intel_newsroom/blog/2013/01/10/intel-announces-groundbreaking-women-and-the-web-report-with-un-women-and-state-department
Accessed on February 21, 2013.

Women and the Web, Intel Cooperation, 2012.
http://www.intel.com/content/dam/www/public/us/en/documents/pdf/women-and-the-web.pdf
Accessed on February 21, 2013.

Supply Side: Monitoring the Gender Impact of e-Government

In order to assess the actual use of services by women, a well-designed monitoring system should be put in place to analyze trends and performance. This technical aspect of outreach should be implemented in coordination with national statistics agencies to ensure data compatibility and to maximize the utilization of data.

[Figure 35] Centralized Model of Gender / e-Gov Database

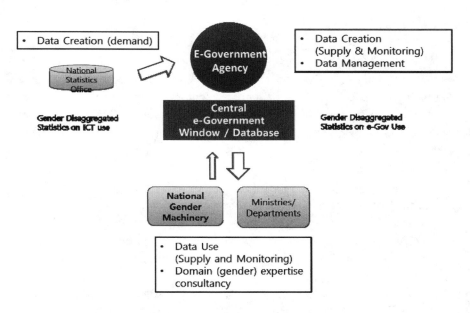

Additional resource links for this step

Category	Resource Type	Title	Publisher	Index Number
Establish a gender database	Policy report	Creating and Sustaining Superior ICT Project Performance Through Gender Sensitivity	USAID	09
	Overview report	Gender and Indicators Overview Report	UNDP	10
	Practice note	Gender Equality Indicators: What, Why and How?	The Organisation for Economic Co-operation and Development (OECD)	11
	Guide	Guide to Gender-Sensitive Indicators	Canadian International Development Agency (CIDA)	12
	Resource collection	Gender and Indicators: Supporting Resources Collection	Institute of Development Studies (IDS) BRIDGE	13
	Policy report	Indicators for Monitoring Gender and ICT	The World Bank	14
	Guide	A User's Guide to Measuring Gender-Sensitive Basic Service Delivery	United Nations Development Programme (UNDP) UN Women	15

Box 14

Open Database for Women's Empowerment: Land Portal and Gender Mapper

Open Data commonly refers to the idea of freely availing certain data for everyone to use and republish. In particular, a growing number of national governments and international organizations have created websites to distribute data for collaborative projects. Open, collaborative and user-driven online platforms encourage dialogue and the sharing of information and good practices around critical issues and have a good potential for generating new knowledge and increasing transparency – and, ultimately, to improve social equity and strengthen democracy.

The Land Portal (http://landportal.info/) is a good example as it acts as an online hub for sharing information and fostering dialogue on land related issues. This is accomplished through a user driven platform which allows users to share information by uploading content, commenting and rating existing information, and retrieving information using specific filters. These two functions- data aggregation and stakeholder dialogue- provide the framework for new partnerships by empowering land-concerned individuals, communities, organizations, practitioners, and policy makers to share perspectives and best practices, and to collaborate strategically.

Gender Mapper (http://gender.mappr.info/) is a gender-focused version of an open data project on land rights issue. The website is provided by The International Food Policy Research Institute (IFPRI) and the International Water Management Institute (IWMI), which hosts a "gender map" of agriculture in Sub-Saharan Africa in order to better understand how to target agricultural interventions to women and men farmers.

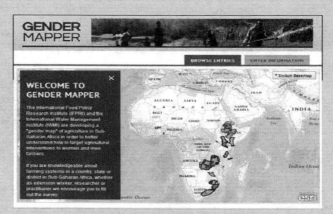

Gender Mapper Website

Alongside the Land Portal, and Gender Mapper, platforms such as Wikigender, e-agriculture, AIMS, FSN-Forum and the Open Development list offer services including list serves, communities of practice and knowledge sharing platforms on the issues of natural resource governance and/or gender equity.

Source: Land Portal Homepage
http://landportal.info/content/using-online-platforms-increase-access-open-data-and-share-best-practices-monitoring-women-s
Accessed on February 13, 2013.

Gender Mapper Homepage
http://gender.mappr.info/explore.php Accessed on February 2, 2013.

4.5   Build Human Capacity

There are two distinct aspects when it comes to capacity building: first, to enhance ICT literacy of women to ensure their equitable access to e-Government initiatives as a traditionally marginalized service recipient; second, to generate and promote the ICT service capacity of government officials and staffs within the national gender machinery as the main provider of e-Government services for women.

Women's ICT Capacity

Promoting women's ICT capacity is a key factor in increasing women's demand for e-Government services. Capacity building happens at two levels – individual and network.

[Figure 36] ICT Capacity Building: Key Considerations

E-Government Supply Side

National Gender Machinery

- Develop, operate and maintain information system
- Procurement of ICT service
- Service delivery, maintenance, and operation
- E-Government programme/ project management
- Change management
- Citizen Relations Management

E-Government Demand Side

Citizen (Women)

- Basic ICT literacy education under school curriculums
- Use of access facilities i.e. telecentres
-

At the individual level, the most frequently referred method is **ICT trainings**. An increasing number of governments started providing ICT education under the formal school system, and as the enrolment ratio of women gradually increased, the benefits of basic ICT education is increasingly reaching out to women. Outside the boundary of formal education, community telecentres play a role to provide access to ICT and serve as training sites to increase ICT capacity.

In addition to technical capacity building, efforts to demystify technologies used for e-Government and information services can lead to greater efficacy with technology and wider participation by women.

At the supporting network level, improving the ICT capacity of women's cooperatives and organizations is important. By bringing offline networks into online spaces, it can be expected there will be stronger and more aware demand base from women NGOs, which may in turn serve as a critical intermediary that connect the last mile between the government online service and women population that is hard-to-reach.

It is also critical to encourage national, regional and local cooperation in terms of **programme and resource sharing.**

Institutional Capacity Building

From the institutional perspective, the scarcity of trained human resources at the national gender machinery is often considered as one of the roadblocks toward establishing an effective e-Government and information service network. It is important to strengthen the ICT capacity of the staff, who have gender programme expertise, so that they understand the process of e-Government development including the ICT needs assessment, system design and implementation, and the possibilities and limitations of such e-Government for greater gender inclusion in the public service. The adequate level of ICT capacity for the staff is a prerequisite to making sure that their programme expertise translates into well-designed e-Government projects, whereas the e-Government initiative serves as an efficient means to an end rather than being an end in itself.

Training areas should include technical issues, content development, and e-Government management among others. Regular training for personnel in the national gender machinery and resource pooling can also ensure the operational sustainability of e-Government initiatives, and is vital to long-term sustainability beyond the initial period of implementation.

Additional resource links for this step

Box 15

Malaysian Women Redefine Gender Roles in Technology

According to Ulf Mellstrom, the author of "Masculinity, Power and Technology: A Malaysian Ethnography", professions in ICT are increasingly seen as "women-friendly." Initially, women left their villages to seek urban opportunities in the electronics industry, where their dexterity and willingness to take on indoor production work created a massive new workforce. As electronics jobs were replaced by technological ones, the field opened up to newly educated women who assumed positions of authority in a field that is non-traditional by nature. The country's decision to build a Multimedia Super Corridor in a special administrative zone facilitated the engagement of women in the ICT sector. The critical mass of women in ICT provides a role model for other women and establishes "a symbolic space" that demonstrated that women can and do excel in the field. And because the ICT boom has caused a critical shortage of well-trained ICT specialists, the country's ICT sector welcomed women as new members of the formerly male-dominated community.

Ruth Schechter, Malaysian women redefine gender roles in technology, Gender News, The Clayman Institute for Gender Research at Stanford University, 2010.
http://gender.stanford.edu/news/2011/malaysian-women-redefine-gender-roles-technology Accessed on January 10, 2013.

Category	Resource Type	Title	Publisher	Index Number
Build Human Capacity	Policy report	Information and Communication Technologies in Bangladesh: Trends, Opportunities and Options for Women Workers	Networked Intelligence for Development (NID)	16
	Web resources	Integrating Gender: Publications	Networked Intelligence for Development (NID)	17

Box 16

Toward a Greater Access to Career Opportunities for Women in ICT Economy

A recent ITU publication *A Bright Future in ICTs: Opportunities for a new generation of women* points out that the emerging ICT ecosystem presents an opportunity to harness its 'equalizing force' to transform the existing economic and social stereotypes that are detrimental to gender equity and equality. Considering that the ICT markets are gradually shifting towards non-OECD economies, governments and private sectors in the Asia Pacific should work together to utilize women as an untapped talent pool for the ICT growth sectors in the region.

ICTs both as a sector in itself and as an enabler of gender-neutral transformation across sectors

There are a number of countries in Asia and the Pacific that already witness an important positive impact of the growth of IT services and IT-enabled services on the status of women. For example in the Philippines, women account for about 65 per cent of the total professional and technical workers in IT services and IT-enabled services (World Bank, 2009). In India, women make up 30 per cent of the IT services and IT-enabled workforce—a much higher rate of female participation than in the services sector in general—and this share is expected to grow to 45 per cent by 2010 (World Bank, 2009). More than half of call center employees are women. In both countries, women fill a greater number of high-paying jobs in IT services and IT-enabled services than in most other sectors of the economy.

The publication suggests several strategic areas for further engagement in the short run. These sectors are most in tune with where women in emerging and developing countries already play a major role, e.g. in health, education, social protection, agriculture and rural development, urban development, infrastructure, environment, and social development, among others.

Attracting women and keeping them

The report states that in order to prepare girls and women for the future workforce in the ICT growth sectors, training and education at three distinct levels are required:

- Entrance levels by way of education, training, recruitment, technology camps and public campaigns, internship and career incentives – which require a national reassessment of educational infrastructure and delivery systems.
- Mid-career levels through career promotion and training – the continued feminization of lower level clerical jobs with a female minority in managerial and technical roles needs to be redressed through a combination of policies designed to enable women to further develop their careers.
- Management and senior levels through mentorship, sponsorship programmes and targeted management quotas

At the same time, parents, teachers, career guidance counselors and recruiters need to shift their own mindsets acknowledging that ICT careers are an important and viable opportunity for girls. And in order to secure initial gains made, women already active in the ICT sector need to take time to engage with community initiatives to mentor girls and young women and participate in virtual, face-to-face communities of practice. This multi-pronged approach must be reflected in national strategies and policy initiatives.

Excerpted from *A Bright Future in ICTs: Opportunities for new generation of women*, ITU, 2012.
http://girlsinict.org/sites/default/files/pages/itu_bright_future_for_women_in_ict-english.pdf
Accessed on February 2, 2013.

4.6   Ensure Technology Access for Women

Providing women with affordable access to ICT infrastructure is crucial to the success of e-Government initiatives for gender inclusion. However, many developing countries still have an insufficient level of telecommunication infrastructure, which poses a threat to an equitable and effective online service delivery to women. In this sense, the choice of **technologies for e-Government** developments should reflect the current level of infrastructure maturity across the country.

Ensure Connectivity with Existing Resources

Countries in the emerging and interacting stages of e-Government development should consider utilizing existing ICT infrastructure such as public kiosks, and public and private facilities to provide crucial connectivity for women. Encouraging women's use of and engagement to community telecentres in remote areas can serve as a cost efficient solution to connectivity issues without consideration of high-cost factors. Such arrangements of gender-equitable access to public ICT infrastructure are best incorporated in a national ICT policy, which outlines the country's long-term investment plans for telecommunication infrastructure development.

Box 17

Empowering Women and Girls Through ICT at Libraries

Girls and women need places where they feel comfortable going to access computers, the Internet, technology training and other applications for example including the e-Government. Public libraries are potentially valuable resource in this regard that could help scale and institutionalize women's and girls' access to ICT, and play a significant role as a hub for economic and social change in developing countries.

According to Beyond Access, a collaborative project of global NGOs and academia supported by Bill & Melinda Gates Foundation, library stakeholders have emerged as strong advocates for comprehensive library and information services for women. Notably, several targeted programs in Africa and Latin America demonstrate promising cases of bridging gender gaps in ICT usage.

For example, the Northern Regional Library in Tamale, Ghana established a programme that provides technology training on Internet, web 2.0. use, and search techniques, along with leadership development workshops. the library instituted training hours to make it easier for girls to attend the training while still working during the day. In addition, the library also provides general computer and Internet access for the community and hosts regular events about ICT, creating a space where females patrons can participate.

For more information, visit Beyond Access homepage.
http://www.beyondaccess.net_

Source: Excerpted from Beyond Access Issue Brief, October 2012.
http://www.beyondaccess.net/2012/10/18/empowering-women-and-girls-through-ict-at-libraries-october-issue-brief/
Accessed on February 21, 2013

Selective Push for an Appropriate Technology for Women: m-Government

Considering the limitation in connectivity that many developing countries still face, policy makers can explore the possibility to selectively "push" an appropriate delivery channel that is most appropriate for effective delivery of online services for women. While choosing an appropriate technology, issues such as access, cost, maintenance, interactivity, user-friendliness, availability and speed should be considered (Baste, 1995). In selecting appropriate technologies for delivery, efficiency may vary in terms of outreach capability, flexibility, interactivity, and other factors (Tobing, 2002).

Despite the disparities in penetration between world regions and countries, mobile cellular phones are the most commonly used ICT in most countries (ITU, 2009). The relatively low cost of hardware and infrastructure deployment cost, combined with the affordable usage rates and mobility, make mobile phones powerful tools for the provision of e-Government service, particularly to women in developing countries and regions without sufficient infrastructure (ITU, 2009).The mobility of the device poses an advantage for women; women can access e-government services even from home, without needing to travel to cybercafés and telecentres in order to access internet-connected computers, when home connection is not available.

In this regard, m-government, the extension of e-Government to mobile platforms, may provide additional advantages for women, particularly regarding emergency response services for domestic violence or other crimes, as shown in the case of Republic of Korea.

Box 18

Aponjon m-Health Service in Bangladesh

"Aponjon" is an m-Health service through mobile phones for expecting and new mothers in Bangladesh. The service provides weekly health messages to expecting and new mothers to encourage proper care during pregnancy and after the baby is born. The low-cost service, free for the poorest 20% of its subscribers, aims to reduce maternal and newborn illnesses and deaths. Aponjon was launched by the Government of Bangladesh in May 2011 under the Mobile Alliance for Maternal Action (MAMA) project, a global public-private partnership between USAID, Johnson & Johnson, mHealth Alliance, United Nations Foundation and BabyCenter. Bangladesh, India, and South Africa were selected as pilot countries under MAMA and, of these three countries, Bangladesh is the first to take mobile health messaging services to national scale under Aponjon.

During the pilot phase of the program, the service reached more than 1,600 new and expectant mothers. D.Net has also partnered with the Access to Information (A2I) program – that provides information and services to improve socio-economic conditions of all Bangladeshis by strengthening existing e-services and developing new ones to strongly support Prime Minister Sheikh Hasina's Vision 2021 of a 'Digital Bangladesh'. MAMA Bangladesh initiative has partnered with organizations such as BRAC, Social Marketing Company (SMC), Smiling Sun Franchise Program (SSFP), MCHIP (through MaMoni Program), and Fair Price International (through InfoLady programme) to implement its outreach operations.

As a public-private partnership, 'Aponjon' relies on a multiple sources of revenue for financial sustainability. Corporate sector in the country came forward to support Aponjon in various forms. Beximco Pharmaceuticals Limited has become the first corporate founding partner, whereas Lal Teer and Rahim Afrooz have also joined Aponjon as corporate partner and corporate.

Excerpted from Aponjon Press Release
www.aponjon.com.bd
Accessed on February 21, 2013

Box 19

Mobile for Women's Empowerment

Recently, we have been witnessing a new movement building with innovative developments in mobile applications for gender empowerment, aimed at increasing women's access to and use of mobile and life-enhancing, value-added services in the developing world. These programs have brought together the knowledge, leadership, and resources of governments, public institutions, corporations, and civil society – which can provide a valuable insight to be applied to the case of e-Government and m-Government development. Selected programmes in mobile development —usually called as m-development-- are listed below.

GSMA's mWomen Programme

The programme is launched in 2010 as a joint partnership of USAID, AusAID and telecomm providers with an aimed to halve the mobile phone gender gap in developing countries. The programme particularly focuses on resource-poor women, who are defined as owning low income, low level of empowerment, and limited access to education, and suffering from social isolation due to limited mobility or remote locations.

The programme has three major objectives: 1) Encourage industry to serve resource-poor women; 2) Increase availability of life-enhancing value-added services; and 3) Promote solutions to women's barriers to usage. The programme aims to achieve these objectives by working with mobile operators, value-added service providers, and other mobile industry members, as well as non-governmental organisations (NGOs) and other international development partners. Target areas of the programme cover countries in the Asia Pacific region, including ongoing projects currently taking place in Indonesia and India. For example, Citizen Centre Enterprises (CCE) project in Tamil Nadu, India, presents a case where a local telecommunication provider introduced women into a mobile value chain and delivered business service through a network of women entrepreneurs.

Source: GSMA mWomen Programme Homepage
http://www.gsma.com/mobilefordevelopment/programmes/mwomen_
Accessed on February 13, 2013.

Mobile Alliance for Maternal Action (MAMA)

MAMA is a public-private partnership launched in May 2011 by founding partners USAID and Johnson & Johnson with supporting partners – the United Nations Foundation, mHealth Alliance and BabyCenter, with an aim to delivering vital health information for new and expectant mothers.

MAMA is delivering mobile health information services in Bangladesh, India and South Africa – countries with elevated maternal and infant mortality and morbidity and high use of mobile phones. MAMA is partnering with local governments, mobile operators and non-government organizations in these countries to ensure from the start that its efforts can be expanded or replicated to reach the most mothers possible. Second, in addition to its collaborative efforts in Bangladesh, India and South Africa, MAMA is also enhancing global capability of agencies that create and develop mobile health information programs for moms. Currently, its first tool, adaptable messages are being used in 35 countries with a goal of reaching 20 million mothers.

Source: MAMA Homepage
http://www.healthunbound.org/mama
Accessed on February 21, 2013

Samasource

Samasource, a U.S. based NGO established in 2008 provides stable, living wages to women through Internet-based work opportunities. Samasource secures contracts from enterprise customers to provide data entry, digitization, content moderation, and other outsourcing services. The work is divided into smaller tasks called "microwork" which are completed by Samasource's distributed workforce. This workforce comes from Service Partners in 6 different countries including Haiti, India, Kenya, Pakistan, South Africa, and Uganda.

Source: Samasource Homepage
http://samasource.org/
Accessed on February 21, 2013

4.7 Define Laws and Policies Pertaining to Women's ICT Use

Formulating appropriate laws and policies that define and guide e-government efforts are a 'must' when it comes to drawing an action plan for gender inclusion in e-Government, since it is crucial for both affordability and sustainability of such initiatives. While many of the legal frameworks in this category, including those that protect and safeguard user information and prevent potential threats of the online space, overlap the general requirement for national e-Government plan, there are several issues that require particular consideration for women.

These legal and regulatory measures would typically pertain to:
- The use of public information by third parties, safeguarding privacy and security issues
- Integrating and sharing data systems within and among administrations to cater to joint services of the government

Safeguarding public information and privacy (ICT misuse education)
Some of the negative changes that are brought to our society by the Internet and other related technologies have made possible new ways of committing violence against women.

Policy makers should recognize the incidents of ICT-related violence, such as cyber stalking or cyber pornography that may arise from the lack of protection on personal data. Laws and regulations to prevent such negative side-effects should be set in place in continuum with national initiatives for gender inclusion in e-Government as a necessary precondition.

In addition, preventive education should be put in place in conjunction with ICT capacity building programmes so that women can understand that protecting privacy and identity online is essential in knowing their rights as ICT users and as women. Practically, the education should include precautionary measures women can take as a responsible ICT user when engaging online service in order to ensure security and safety.

Key recommendations in this area may include (adapted from APC, 2010):
- be aware of women's rights and know that these rights are to be respected, protected and fulfilled even in an online environment
- raise awareness of women to be vigilant when participating online to ensure safety and privacy
- build and promote networks and organize online campaigns to combat violence against women for public
- form task forces to monitor violations online
- provide channels to document and report online violations
- create hotlines and set up interactive websites where women can ask and answer questions and respond to victims of online violence.

System Integration for Gender Mainstreaming in e-Governance

Depending on the level of e-Government technological advancement, countries may choose the most relevant form of e-Government programmes for a greater gender inclusion, either through the website of the national gender machinery, national portal of e-Government, or social networks and other established online-based services. While the choice should be based on promoting the usability, ease of use and convenience for e-Government programmes for women, it is important to make sure that the system and services are seamlessly integrated with a single national e-Government window in the long run.

- Database including gender-disaggregated usage, level of satisfaction, and impact
- System interface integrating gender-specific services and general services
- Process re-engineering to reflect gender-sensitive programme design, implementation and monitoring

Additional resource links for this step

Category	Resource Type	Title	Publisher	Index Number
Define laws and policies	Policy report	Considerations for Gender Advocacy vis-à-vis ICT Policy and Strategy	InfoDev Program World Bank	19
	Policy report	PAN Evaluations : Gender Integration and Policy Influence	International Development Research Centre (IDRC)	20
	Policy report	Trend and Status of Gender Perspectives in ICT Sector: Case Studies in Asia and the Pacific Countries	International Telecommunication Union (ITU)	21
	Policy report	Critically absent: women's rights in internet governance	APC	22
	Policy report	APC Policy Monitor in Latin America and the Caribbean, 2008, Cybercrime laws are not enough, there is also a need for education	APC	23

4.8   Establish a Network of Partners

Collaboration is the key for an e-government drive for a greater gender inclusion that encompasses issues of gender development and ICT/e-Government and seeks to transform the process of gender-related public service as a whole. It is suggested to form a network of partners that comprise organizations and agencies that can effectively assist and participate in the implementation of e-government for gender inclusion initiatives.

Collaboration with NGOs

NGOs are among a highly active segment of society in most developing countries and they normally focus their activities in specific areas of community development, particularly including gender equality. As such, NGOs enjoy a high trust level with local women groups. These organizations can play a key role by voicing the needs of the community of local women before the government and assisting them in the policy making process of e-Government initiatives for gender inclusion. In addition, NGOs specialized in ICT enabled social services can provide insight as to the selection of appropriate technology, system design and service delivery over the Internet. Last but not least, NGOs can act as an important channel for not only promoting e-Government initiatives among women and the masses, but also spreading awareness about the benefits and usage of online government services, as well as the imperatives for greater gender inclusion in the information society as a whole.

Box 20

Gender and Citizenship: CITIGEN Collaboration Project

In 2010, IT for Change, supported by the International Development Research Centre (IDRC), undertook a two-year small grants programme – 'Gender and citizenship in the information society' (CITIGEN) to explore how the citizenship of marginalised women in the global South had evolved in the emergent techno-social paradigm. Its additional objectives were to examine the challenges to and opportunities for women's citizenship as they are shaped by new ICTs in relation to specific social and institutional ecologies; to propose ways forward for practice and policy in relation to information and communication domains that place women's citizenship at the centre, and; to build a network of researchers, scholars and policy makers on information society and gender issues in Asia.

Women-gov is another feminist action-research project supported by IDRC, which aims at enhancing marginalised women's active citizenship and their engagement with local governance. The research project is being conducted across three sites in India, Brazil and South Africa, in partnership with IT for Change in India, Instituto Nupef in Brazil and the New Women's Movement in South Africa.

At each of the three sites, the project developed a sustainable techno-social intervention model for enabling marginalised women's collectives to enhance their active engagement with governance structures and the collective articulation and negotiation of their interests; and build peer-to-peer networks for increasing their political participation. In short, exploring the conditions for women's active citizenship, a precondition for effective participatory governance, through digital technologies is the central concern of the project.

Source: CITIGEN project homepage at
http://www.gender-is-citizenship.net/
Accessed on February 21, 2013

Setting up of Research and Training Institutes

These institutes are proven to be helpful in conducting the e-readiness assessment studies with a focus on gender divide, policy analysis and research on possible e-Government applications for women, technological issues, data requirements, regulatory reforms and how G-government can facilitate gender empowerment and sustainable development. Institutions working in the area of gender development, public administration, government services training and other ICT training institutes can play an important role in capacity building within the government.

Partnership with International Organizations

International agencies including those under the United Nations system can act as important partners for e-government initiatives for gender inclusion, as they play a facilitating role in not only raising the awareness and advocating for e-government and gender advancement, but also by stimulating international discussion and exchange of good practices. Regional cooperation organizations, particularly including ASEAN and APEC in Asia and the Pacific region, can also provide assistance in this regard, with an advantage of specific regional focus. Areas of cooperation include joint research, seminars and workshops for government officials, financial resources as well as technical expertise.

Box 21

PRIDE project – ICT programmes for small Pacific island states

The Project is a collaborative partnership implemented by the Institute of Education at the University of the South Pacific, jointly funded by the European Union (EU) through the European Development Fund (EDF) and New Zealand through New Zealand Agency for International Development (NZAID). The primary aims of the project is to enhance the capacity of Pacific education agencies to effectively plan and deliver quality basic education through formal and non-formal means, and to improve the coordination of donor inputs to assist countries implement their plans.

The project serves small Pacific island states including Cook Islands, Federated States of Micronesia, Fiji, Kiribati, Marshall Islands, Nauru, Niue, Palau, Papua New Guinea, Samoa, Solomon Islands, Tokelau, Tonga, Tuvalu and Vanuatu. Particularly through workshops and knowledge sharing programs, the project has been contributing to strengthen access to resources and information literacy for all students including girls. Examples of PRIDE project include Community Awareness Work shop and Adult Education, Establishment of Distance Education Centres, and Teacher/Librarian-Train the Trainers in Fiji.

Primarily from the angle of an educational cooperation, the project presents an example of a regional partnership aimed at increasing the ICT human capacity in the region and a possibility of utilizing a higher education institute i.e. universities as a hub for human and technical exchanges.

Excerpted from *A Bright Future in ICTs: Opportunities for new generation of women*, ITU, 2012., p.33.
Original Source:
PRIDE Project homepage, The University of the South Pacific
www.usp.ac.fj/index.php?id=pride_home0
Accessed on January 10, 2013

4.9   Identify & Implement Pilot Projects

With the stage set, the next step is to identify projects that will lead the way and set examples, as well as provide important lessons for the future of a greater gender inclusion in e-Government. Selecting the right project to be the 'pilot' is very important, since a successful project becomes a powerful selling point for all future efforts and creates the necessary political momentum needed to move the initiative ahead. Such projects also help in generating demand from women for more of such initiatives.

For choosing pilot projects, it is suggested to involve major stakeholders and build a consensus. An assessment of the current state of gender concerns in public administration, ICT implementation and resources in various sectors can be carried out to act as a foundation for selecting possible pilot projects.

[Figure 37] Potential e-Government Project Areas

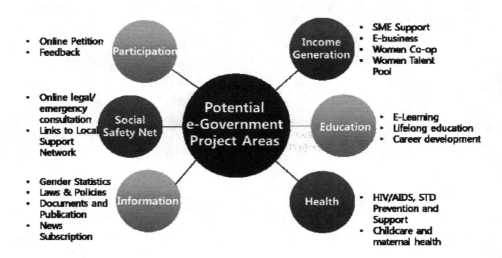

A list of potential projects can also be selected by inviting proposals from different departments. Since the objective is to ensure success for the pilot project and not to spend resources in reinventing the wheel, it will also be advisable to borrow ideas from other regions or countries that have successfully implemented similar projects. Many countries have developed evaluation frameworks to prioritize and select those projects that offer a high value at a comparatively low risk.

The following points must be kept in consideration while identifying a pilot project for implementation:
- The goal of the project is consistent with the overall vision
- The identified segment of gender issue is a priority area and possesses a positive culture for adopting good practices
- The identified pilot project is one that directly benefits a large number of women

Additional resource links for this step

Category	Resource Type	Title	Publisher	Index Number
Conduct a Pilot	Toolkit	Toward Gender Equality in Europe and Eurasia: a Toolkit for Analysis	USAID	23
	Book	Gender and ICTs for Development: A Global Sourcebook	Royal Tropical Institute (KIT), The Netherlands & Oxfam GB	24
	Academic article	E-government and Gender Digital Divide: The Case of Jordan	International Journal of Electronic Business Management (IJEBM)	25

Box 22

GenADRIS Grant Programme for Innovative Project

Women in rural areas play a central role in the agricultural economy of their region, which means that they often work long hours, leaving little time for learning how to use new technologies Yet, access to new technologies affect both men and women in remote areas.

The Gender, Agriculture and Rural Development in the Information Society (GenARDIS) small grants fund was initiated in 2002 to support work on gender-related issues in ICT for the African, Caribbean and Pacific regions. The small grants fund was disbursed to diverse and innovative projects in order to counter these barriers, to document the process and results, and to contribute to more gender-aware ICT policy advocacy.

For more information on the project, visit GenADRIS homepage
http://genardis.apcwomen.org/en/news_interviews

Source: GenADRIS 2002-2010: Small Grants that made big changes for women in agriculture, Association for Progressive Communications (APC), 2010
http://www.apc.org/en/system/files/Genardis_EN.pdf
accessed on February 13, 2013.

5. Conclusion

In the knowledge society, e-Government presents an opportunity to improve public service delivery as well as to broaden the range of opportunities for citizens to participate in the public decision-making process. However, this opportunity also presents the challenge of inclusiveness that is already prevalent in ICT access and use. The lack of representation from marginalized groups, particularly women who still suffer from gendered aspects of the digital divide in many countries, can further marginalize these groups from government service provision and participation. It is crucial to develop e-Government strategies targeted specifically towards empowerment of women if the digital divide is to be closed.

While limited in their generalizability, the policy surveys and e-Government readiness index for gender equality of national operations for gender development in eleven selected countries demonstrated that e-Government provisions for women still remain an emerging policy issue, which warrant more attention from national governments. This report identified the modules of policy recommendations that reflect the range of different country contexts regarding the country's gender development goals, e-Government sophistication and ICT infrastructure.

At the analysis level, this report has discussed why governments should take proactive initiatives to provide women-specific services. Additionally, at the design and implementation level, the following points have been made as research findings and recommendations:

- Many programmes designed to increase women's ICT adoption fail due to the lack of relevant content for women
- e-Government adoption depends on the ease of use as well as usefulness of service and content
- This "usefulness" should increase, with sites providing richer and more relevant content and services, as well as multiple ways to access content
- As the services expand, it is critical to encourage women to participate in decision-making in the public sphere, so that their needs are recognized and considered.
- To develop a national level action plan, the following steps can be considered: 1) define national vision 2) raise awareness, 3) establish a focal organization, 4) establish a gender database, 5) build human capacity, 6) ensure technology access, 7) define laws and policies, 8) establish partnerships, and 9) conduct pilot projects

It is only through increased participation that e-Government can be sustained and scale to have greater impact on women's development.

6. References

Alampay, G. & Umali, J., 2007. *High Impact, Pro-Poor e-Governance Applications: Identifying 'Killer Applications' and Best Practice Models of e-Governance through Community e-Centers in the Philippines,* s.l.: UNDP Philippines /UNDP-APDIP.

AL-Rababah, B. A. & Abu-Shanab, E. A., 2010 (Vol 8 No1). E-GOVERNMENT AND GENDER DIGITAL DIVIDE: THE CASE OF JORDAN. *International Journal of Electronic Business Management,* pp. 1-8.

Anon., n.d. *ICTs in Bangladesh Trends and Future Options for Women Workers,* s.l.: s.n.

APC, 2010. *GenADRIS 2002-2010: Small Grants that made big changes for women in agriculture,* Association for Progressive Communications. [Online]
Available at: http://www.apc.org/en/system/files/Genardis_EN.pdf
[Accessed 13 February 2013].

Avgerou, C., 2010. Discourses on ICT and Development. *Information Technologies and International Development,* 6(3), pp. 1-18.

Baste, A., 1995. *Technology, open learning and distance education.* London: Rutledge.

Basu, S., 2004. E-government and developing countries: an overview. *International Review of Law, Computers & Technology,* 18(1), pp. 109-132.

Bell, E., & Esplenm E. 2007. *Gender and Indicators: Supporting Resources Collection,* Institute of Development Studies (IDS) BRIDGE. [Online]
Available at:
http://www.bridge.ids.ac.uk/go/bridge-publications/cutting-edge-packs/gender-and-indicators/gender-and-indicators&id=54158&type=Document&langid=1
[Accessed 13 July 2012]

Betancourt, V., 2006. *E-government: An opportunity for citizen participation in the era of digital development.* [Online]
Available at:
http://www.apc.org/en/news/all/world/e-government-opportunity-citizen-participation-era
[Accessed 28 November 2011].

Beyond Access, 2012. *Empowering women and girls through ICT at libraries,* Beyond Access Issue Brief, October 2012. [Online]
Available at:
http://www.beyondaccess.net/2012/10/18/empowering-women-and-girls-through-ict-at-libraries-october-issue-brief/
[Accessed 21 February 2013]

China National Programme for Women's Development 2011-2020. People's Daily Online. [Online]
Available at: http://politics.people.com.cn/h/2011/0808/c226651-2249608525.html
[Accessed 3 March 2013].

CIA, n.d. *The World Fact Book.* [Online]
Available at:
https://www.cia.gov/library/publications/the-world-factbook/geos/tt.html
[Accessed 17 November 2011].

Demetriades, J., 2009. *Gender Equality Indicators: What, Why and How?,* The Organisation for Economic Co-operation and Development (OECD). [Online]
Available at: http://www.oecd.org/social/genderequalityanddevelopment/44952761.pdf
[Accessed 13 July 2012]

Dorner, D. G., 2006. Information Literacy Education in Asian Developing Countries: cultural factors affecting curriculum development and programme delivery. *IFLA Journal,* 32(4), pp. 281-293.

Gurumurthy, A., Nandini, C., & Saloranta, E. 2013. *Through the 'information society' prism: Scoping gender equality for the post-2015 agenda,* wICT4D conference Position Paper, IT for Change. [Online]
Availabe at:
http://www.itforchange.net/sites/default/files/ITfC/Through%20the%20information%20society%20pris
m%20-%20Scoping%20gender%20equality%20for%20the%20post-2015%20agenda.pdf
[Accessed February 10 2013].

Hafkin, N., 2003. *Some thoughts on gender and telecommunications/ICT statistics and indicators,* Geneva: ITU.

Hafkin, N. & Huyer, S., 2007. *Engendering the Knowledge Society: measuring women's participation,* Montreal: ORBICOM.

Hausmann, R., Tyson L. D., & Zahidi, S., 2011. The Global Gender Gap Report 2011, Geneva: World Economic Forum. [Online]
http://www3.weforum.org/docs/WEF_GenderGap_Report_2011.pdf
[Accessed 3 March 2012].

Heeks, R., 2001. *Understanding e-Governance for Development, i-Government Working Papers.* [Online]
Available at:
http://www.sed.manchester.ac.uk/idpm/research/publications/wp/igovernment/igov_wp11.htm [Accessed 28 November 2011].

Hijab, N., & Zambrano, R., 2008. *Gender Responsive E-governance: Exploring the Transformative Potential,* New York: United Nations Development Programme.
Available at:
http://www.undp.org/content/undp/en/home/librarypage/womens-empowerment/primers-in-gender-and-democratic-governance-4.html
[Accessed 13 July 2012]

Hussain, F. & Tongia, R., 2010. A framework and case example for evaluating cost-effectiveness of information services across technologies. *Information Technologies and International Development,* 6(2), pp. 55-74.

IAMAI, 2012. *Internet in Rural India,* Delhi: Internet and Mobile Association of India.

Intel Cooperation, 2012. *Women and the Web,* Intel Corporation [Online]
Available at:
http://www.intel.com/content/dam/www/public/us/en/documents/pdf/women-and-the-web.pdf
[Accessed 21 February 2013].

ITU, 2009. *e-Government Readiness Assessment Framework,* s.l.: ITU.

ITU, 2010. *ITU Statistics by gender.* [Online]
Available at: http://www.itu.int/ITU-D/ict/statistics/Gender/index.html
[Accessed 16 November 2011].

ITU, 2011. Measuring the Information Society, Geneva: International Telecommunication Union. [Online]
Available at: http://www.itu.int/net/pressoffice/backgrounders/general/pdf/5.pdf
[Accessed 22 December 2012].

ITU, 2012. A Bright Future in ICTs: Opportunities for new generation of women, Geneva:ITU. [Online]
Available at:
http://girlsinict.org/sites/default/files/pages/itu_bright_future_for_women_in_ict-english.pdf
[Accessed 2 February 2013].

Korea Women's Development Institute, 2011. *Gender Statistics Information System* [Online].
Available at http://gsis.kwdi.re.kr/gsis/eg/main.html
[Accessed 3 March 2013].

Molnár, S. *The Explanation Frame of the Digital Divide*, Proceedings of the Summer School, "Risks and Challenges of the Network Society" (Karlstad University, Sweden) [Online].
Available at: http://www.academia.edu/1308255/The_explanation_frame_of_the_digital_divide
[Accessed 3 March 2013].

Morgan, S., Heeks, R., & Arun, S., 2004. *Researching ICT-Based Enterprise for Women in Developing Countries: A Gender Perspective*, Institute for Development Policy and Management (IDPM), University of Manchester, UK.
Available at: http://www.dfid.gov.uk/r4d/PDF/Outputs/ICT/R8352-GenderResearch.pdf
[Accessed 13 July 2012]

Moser, A., 2007. *Gender and Indicators Overview Report*, United Nations Development Programme (UNDP).
Available at:
http://www.undp.org/content/dam/aplaws/publication/en/publications/poverty-reduction/poverty-website/gender-and-indicators/GenderandIndicators.pdf
[Accessed 13 July 2012]

NASSCOM, 2010. Impact of IT-BPO Industry in India: A Decade in Review. pp. 12-13;

Ndou, V., 2004. E-Government for developing countries: opportunities and challenges. *Electronic Journal on Information Systems in Developing Countries,* 18(1), pp. 1-24.
publication, I. 2., n.d. [Online]
Available at:
http://www.itu.int/ITU-D/ict/publications/idi/2011/Material/MIS_2011_ without_annex_5.pdf

Sachdeva, N., Peebles, D., 2010. *PAN Evaluations: Gender Integration and Policy Influence*, International Development Research Centre (IDRC) [Online].
Available at: http://idl-bnc.idrc.ca/dspace/handle/10625/45401
[Accessed 13 July 2012]

Tandon, N., 2006. *Information and Communication Technologies in Bangladesh; Trends, Opportunities and Options for Women Worker,* s.l.: Networked Intelligence for Development.

Tobing, L., 2002. *How to do community radio: a primer for community radio operators.* New Delhi: UNESCO.

UN DESA, 2002. *Information and Communication Technologies and Their Impact on and Use as an Instrument for the Advancement and Empowerment of Women*, The United Nations Division for the Advancement of Women Department of Economic and Social Affairs (UNDAW/DESA). [Online]
Available at: http://www.un.org/womenwatch/daw/egm/ict2002/reports/EGMFinalReport.pdf

[Accessed 13 July 2012]

UN DESA, 2010. *United Nations e-Government Survey 2010: Leveraging e-Government at a time of financial and economic crisis,* New York: United Nations Department of Economic and Social Affairs. [Online] Available at: http://unpan1.un.org/intradoc/groups/public/documents/un/unpan038851.pdf [Accessed 22 December 2012].

UN DESA, 2012. *United Nations e-Government Survey 2012: e-Government for the People*, New York: United Nations Department of Economic and Social Affairs. [Online] Available at: http://www2.unpan.org/egovkb/global_reports/12report.htm [Accessed 22 December 2012].

UNESCO, 2005. *E-Government Toolkit for Developing Countries,* New Delhi: UNESCO. [Online] Available at http://unesdoc.unesco.org/images/0013/001394/139418e.pdf [Accessed 2 March 2013].

UNFPA, 2012. *Gender Equality: Empowering Women* [Online] Available at: http://www.unfpa.org/gender/empowerment.htm [Accessed 2 March 2013].

United Nations, 1995. *Beijing Declaration.* [Online] Available at: http://www.un.org/womenwatch/daw/beijing/platform/declar.htm [Accessed 16 November 2011].

United Nations, 2000. *United Nations Millennium Declaration.* [Online] Available at: http://www.un.org/millennium/declaration/ares552e.pdf [Accessed 18 November 2011].

United Nations, 2010. *Information and communications technology and gender equality: new opportunities and challenges for public administration to implement the internationally agreed development goals, including the Millennium Development Goals,* New York: United Nations Economic and Social Council, Committee of Experts on Public Administration.

Valk, M., Cummings, S.J.R. & Van Dam, H., 2005. *Gender and ICTs for Development: A Global Sourcebook,* Royal Tropical Institute (KIT), The Netherlands & Oxfam GB [Online] Available at: http://www.unapcict.org/ecohub/resources/gender-and-icts-for-development-a-global-sourcebook [Accessed 13 July 2012]

Women Digital Literacy Programme 2011. *Empowering Women in Rural India through Digital Literacy*, Common Services Centers Scheme, Department of Electronics and Information Technology, Government of India. [Online] Available at: http://csc.gov.in/index.php?option=com_content&view=article&id=180&Itemid=347 [Accessed 3 March 2013].

World Bank, 2008. *Checklist for the Planning, Design and Implementation of an ICT Project Incorporating Gender Issues.* [Online] Available at http://go.worldbank.org/8EHJW80CY0 [Accessed 13 July 2012]

World Bank, 2009. *Definition of e-Government.* [Online] Available at: http://go.worldbank.org/M1JHE0Z280 [Accessed 16 November 2011].

Annex A: Toolkit Resources

Vision Statement

01

Gender Responsive E-governance: Exploring the Transformative Potential
Nadia Hijab; Raúl Zambrano. UNDP. 2008

URL

http://www.undp.org/content/dam/aplaws/publication/en/publications/womens-empowerment/primers-in-gender-and-democratic-governance-4/f_GenderGovPr_eG_Web.pdf

Purpose

To contribute to the broader discussion of gender and e-governance and facilitate gender responsive e-governance programming by UNDP practitioners and their partners

Intended user

UNDP practitioners and their partners

Available language(s)

English and Arabic

Description

This primer builds on an extensive body of work on ICTs and gender, but focuses on key gender issues related to e-governance within the context of UNDP's work on democratic governance.

These key issues are: (1) policy-making processes for e-governance planning; (2) delivery of basic services and public information via ICTs; and (3) empowerment of stakeholders, particularly women, to use ICT networks to engage with governments over governance processes.

The primer has four sections: Section 1 is an overview of the intersection between ICT, gender and e-governance and UNDP's mandate in regards to this field; Section 2 presents the work UNDP has done to date in integrating these areas; Section 3 builds on the previous sections and highlights key gender considerations for e-governance programming, including major obstacles; and Section 4 presents entry points for continued programming on gender and e-governance, and makes recommendations for closing the existing gender gap in specific e-governance interventions.

02

Checklist for the Planning, Design and Implementation of an ICT Project Incorporating Gender Issues
The World Bank

URL
http://go.worldbank.org/8EHJW80CY0

Purpose
To provide strategic guidance and tools for gender and ICT programs and encourage project planners to consider opportunities that may have been overlooked

Intended user
ICT programme and project creators

Available language(s)
English

Description
This checklist is based on both general principles of gender analysis that are common to all project design, implementation, and ICT-specific issues. Although gender analysis has become an accepted part of most development interventions, it is still a rarity in ICT for development projects. Therefore, the gender analysis of ICT projects involves the application of general principles of gender analysis as well as gender considerations specific to ICTs

03

Gender and ICT

The World Bank

United Nations Development Programme – Asia-Pacific Development Information Programme (UNDP-APDIP)

URL

http://www.unapcict.org/ecohub/resources/gender-and-ict

Purpose

To provide a gender-focused perspective to the issues of ICT policies; access and control; education, training and skill development; content development, and to introduce a framework of gender mainstreaming in ICT for development and women empowerment

Intended user

Policy-makers and Governments

Available language(s)

English

Description

This publication examines and discusses the context of ICTs and gender by placing it within the Gender Equality Framework. The publication will move the dialogue forward to address the questions of implications of integrating a gender perspective by realistically examining the state of play across the region.

Define National Vision

04

ICT and Gender Equality: New Opportunities and Challenges for Public Administration to Implement the Internationally Agreed Development Goals, including the Millennium Development Goals

United Nations Economic and Social Council (UNECOSOC)

URL

http://unpan1.un.org/intradoc/groups/public/documents/un-dpadm/unpan037850.pdf

Purpose

To address practical considerations about the application of ICT in public administration and governance to help women gain access to government information, participate in decision-making and receive social services

Intended user

Government and Policy-makers

Available language(s)

English

Raise Awareness

05

Engendering ICT Toolkit: Challenges and Opportunities for Gender-Equitable Development
The World Bank

URL
http://go.worldbank.org/RGBLRHGVG0

Purpose
To identify opportunities, highlight innovative projects and activities, and suggest how development agencies can help realize the potential for gender equality

Intended user
Policy-makers and Governments

Available language(s)
English

Description
This toolkit can be used to assist developing countries in improving the efficiency and equity of their ICT policies and programmes by ensuring that they respond to the needs of both women and men. The toolkit is divided into 10 sections and it contains checklists, evaluation tools, examples of good practices, and resources that can be used to incorporate gender into ICT projects and project components. The toolkit has been designed for general distribution to researchers, educators, and development practitioners.

Raise Awareness

06

Information and Communication Technologies and Their Impact on and Use as an Instrument for the Advancement and Empowerment of Women

The United Nations Division for the Advancement of Women
Department of Economic and Social Affairs (UNDAW/DESA)

URL

http://www.un.org/womenwatch/daw/egm/ict2002/reports/EGMFinalReport.pdf

Purpose

To examine how the rapid diffusion of ICT and associated growth of the ICT sector offers vast opportunities as well as to pose particular challenges and risks to women's empowerment and promotion of gender equality globally, and especially in developing and transition countries

Intended user

Policy-makers, Governments, CSOs and ICT programme and project creators

Available language(s)

English

Description

The report shows that when there is an enabling environment, ICT can provide diverse avenues for women's social, political and economic empowerment. However, the report will also show that although some national governments, women's NGOs, private sector companies, and the international community have implemented programmes and projects that expand the ability of women to fully enjoy and acquire equitable access to these opportunities, there is still room for considerable improvement to be made.

Establish a Focal Organization

07

Researching ICT-Based Enterprise for Women in Developing Countries: A Gender Perspective
Institute for Development Policy and Management (IDPM)
Sharon Morgan; Richard Heeks; Shoba Arun.
University of Manchester, UK. 2004

URL

http://www.dfid.gov.uk/r4d/PDF/Outputs/ICT/R8352-GenderResearch.pdf

Purpose

To describe the form that a gender perspective to research into ICT-based enterprises for women should take

Intended user

Program evaluators and Researchers

Available language(s)

English

Description

This paper will begin by discussing what a gender perspective implies and various approaches that may be employed. It then outlines the Gender Evaluation Methodology (GEM) (APC-WNSP 2002a), a framework for evaluating gender impacts of ICTs and, lastly, discusses the operationalisation issues of this framework.

Establish a Focal Organization

08

Evaluation of Gender Mainstreaming in UNDP

United Nations Development Programme (UNDP)

2006.

URL

http://web.undp.org/evaluation/documents/eo_gendermainstreaming.pdf

Purpose

To assess the overall performance of UNDP in gender mainstreaming and the promotion of gender equality, and to take stock of what UNDP has done to install gender mainstreaming policies and ensure their implementation in the past ten years

Intended user

Program evaluators and Researchers

Available language(s)

English

Description

The evaluation assessed the overall performance of UNDP in gender mainstreaming and the promotion of gender equality over the past decade, as a means to understand what has and what has not worked, and to guide UNDP in strengthening its strategies and approach in the future. The thrust of this report is therefore to identify what actions are needed to ensure that UNDP moves expeditiously toward effective gender mainstreaming that contributes to improved human development – that is, development that both enhances gender equality and removes gender-related impediments to social, economic, and environmentally sound development.

Establish a Gender Database

09

Creating and Sustaining Superior ICT Project Performance Through Gender Sensitivity
United States Agency for International Development (USAID)
Janice Brodman. USAID. 2005.

URL
http://pdf.usaid.gov/pdf_docs/PNADN054.pdf

Purpose
To assist development professionals to ensure gender sensitivity in ICT activities to ensure gender sensitivity in ICT activities

Intended user
Program evaluators and Researchers

Available language(s)
English

Description
The report consists three parts:
I. Guidelines: concise principles for incorporating gender sensitivity
II. Resources: specific and detailed tools, models and examples, which help the user apply the guidelines.
III. References: organizations, websites, and other sources of potential partners, grantees and expertise worldwide

Establish a Gender Database

10

Gender and Indicators Overview Report

United Nations Development Programme (UNDP)

Annalise Moser. UNDP. 2007.

URL

http://www.undp.org/content/dam/aplaws/publication/en/publications/poverty-reduction/poverty-website/gender-and-indicators/GenderandIndicators.pdf

Purpose

To recommend better utilization and modifications to the gender goals and indices

Intended user

Development agencies, Governments (Gender Ministries), Statisticians, Donors and Researchers

Available language(s)

English

Description

This Overview Report examines conceptual and methodological approaches to gender and measurements of change with a focus on indicators, examining current debates and good practice from the grassroots to the international levels.

Establish a Gender Database

11

Gender Equality Indicators: What, Why and How?

The Organisation for Economic Co-operation and Development (OECD)

Justina Demetriades. OECD. 2009.

URL

http://www.oecd.org/social/genderequalityanddevelopment/44952761.pdf

Purpose

To introduce gender equality indicators as a way of measuring change

Intended user

Government officials and Statisticians

Available language(s)

English

Description

This practice note asks: what are indicators, and why should we develop indicators to measure gender equality? It also addresses the often political issue of what we should be measuring, provides some broad principles that can be applied, and suggests some questions donors can ask when developing gender equality indicators.

Establish a Gender Database

12

Guide to Gender-Sensitive Indicators

Canadian International Development Agency (CIDA)

Minister of Public Works and Government Services Canada. 1997.

URL

http://www.acdi-cida.gc.ca/INET/IMAGES.NSF/vLUImages/Policy/$file/WID-GUID-E.pdf

Purpose

To promote conceptual and methodological understanding of indicators, with a special emphasis on gender-sensitive indicators and to offer suggestions and guidance for the use of gender-sensitive indicators, with a particular focus on projects with an end-user focus.

Intended user

Project level staffs in the Agency working with indicators

Available language(s)

English

Description

This Guide explains why gender-sensitive indicators are useful tools for measuring the results of CIDA's development initiatives. It concentrates in particular on projects with an end-user focus, and shows how gender-sensitive indicators can and should be used in both gender integrated and WID-specific projects, and in combination with other evaluation techniques.

Establish a Gender Database

13

Gender and Indicators: Supporting Resources Collection

Institute of Development Studies (IDS) BRIDGE

E. Bell; E. Esplen. IDS. 2007.

URL

http://www.bridge.ids.ac.uk/go/bridge-publications/cutting-edge-packs/gender-and-indicators/gender-and-indicators&id=54158&type=Document&langid=1

Purpose

To provide a comprehensive overview of conceptual and methodological approaches to gender and measurements of change with a focus on indicators, highlighting good practice from the grassroots level to the international level.

Intended user

Gender and non-gender specialists, Program planners

Available language(s)

English

Description

This collection outlines good practice examples; provides case studies; and summarises toolkits designed to facilitate advocacy, programming and training. It also lists databases of gender statistics and provides networking and contact details of organisations working on gender and related indicators. This collection forms part of the Cutting Edge Pack on Gender and Indicators.

Establish a Gender Database

14

Indicators for Monitoring Gender and ICT

The World Bank

URL

http://go.worldbank.org/VDY0ST50Y0

Purpose

To identify specific indicators for monitoring gender and ICTs and focuses on sex-disaggregated statistics

Intended user

Policy-makers and ICT programme and project creators

Available language(s)

English

Description

The major reason for collecting and disseminating macro-level ICT statistics and indicators by gender is to inform national policy and to set international policy goals. Without data, there is no visibility; without visibility, there is no priority. From both observations and anecdotal evidence, we "know" that there is a gender gap in the digital divide in several developed and many more developing countries, but there is very little data. Without such data, it is difficult, if not impossible to make the case for the inclusion of gender issues in ICT policies, plans and strategies for policymakers. On the project level, the major reason for collecting sex-disaggregated data is to ascertain by measurement if men and women are benefiting differently from project interventions and to take corrective action if this turns out to be the case.

Establish a Gender Database

15

A User's Guide to Measuring Gender-Sensitive Basic Service Delivery
United Nations Development Programme (UNDP)
UN Women

URL

http://www.undp.org/content/undp/en/home/librarypage/democratic-governance/oslo_governance_centre/governance_assessments/a-users-guide-to-measuring-gender-sensitive-basic-service-delivery-1.html

Purpose

To contribute to the development and more effective use of gender-sensitive indicators so that services are delivered more efficiently and effectively to women

Intended user

Government departments, Local governments and NGOs involved in developing, funding and implementing service delivery programmes and End-users of the services (Women)

Available language(s)

English

Description

The Guide aims to help national stakeholders as well as donors and international actors involved in service delivery measurements and programs to improve the measurements of basic services delivery in various areas of governance. The primary focus is on whether the processes that define, generate and deliver the services are sensitive to differences in the needs and situations of women and girls compared to men and boys. It focuses on the processes of governance rather than just the outcomes of governance because it believes that implementation processes are keys to improving the delivery of basic services.

Build Human Capacity

16

Information and Communication Technologies in Bangladesh: Trends, Opportunities and Options for Women Workers

Networked Intelligence for Development (NID)

Nidhi Tandon. NID. 2006.

URL

http://unpan1.un.org/intradoc/groups/public/documents/apcity/unpan038251.pdf

Purpose

To provide a three dimensional framework of recommendations that outline principles of engagement with ICTs; gender specific activities that address structural constraints faced by women, and the macro level gender-mainstreaming policies required to secure and underpin these activities

Intended user

Government and Policy-makers

Available language(s)

English

Description

It concentrates on the main issues relating to women's access to, use and appropriation of ICT tools in the labor market and in self-employment in Bangladesh and determines what strategic options could be pursued to improving their access – under the broad assumption that lacking access to these technologies is detrimental to women's participation in the knowledge economy in the long run.

Build Human Capacity

17

Integrating Gender: Publications

USAID

URL

http://transition.usaid.gov/our_work/cross-cutting_programs/wid/gender/pubs.html

Purpose

To provide a comprehensive reference point for policy makers and programme staff in gender development

Intended user

Government and Policy-makers, programme staff

Available language(s)

English

Ensure Technology Access

18

Information and Communication Technologies in Bangladesh: Trends, Opportunities and Options for Women Workers
Networked Intelligence for Development (NID)
Nidhi Tandon. NID. 2006.

URL

http://unpan1.un.org/intradoc/groups/public/documents/apcity/unpan038251.pdf

Purpose

To provide a three dimensional framework of recommendations that outline principles of engagement with ICTs; gender specific activities that address structural constraints faced by women, and the macro level gender-mainstreaming policies required to secure and underpin these activities

Intended user

Government and Policy-makers

Available language(s)

English

Description

It concentrates on the main issues relating to women's access to, use and appropriation of ICT tools in the labor market and in self-employment in Bangladesh and determines what strategic options could be pursued to improving their access – under the broad assumption that lacking access to these technologies is detrimental to women's participation in the knowledge economy in the long run.

Define Laws and Policies

19

Considerations for Gender Advocacy vis-à-vis ICT Policy and Strategy
Louise Chamberlain. InfoDev Program
World Bank. 2002

URL

http://www.un.org/womenwatch/daw/egm/ict2002/reports/Paper%20by%20Chamberlain.PDF

Purpose
To provide practical guidance for gender advocacy in the ICT policy environment

Intended user
Gender advocates and Policy-makers

Available language(s)
English

Description
The paper discusses ICT policy from the practitioner's view and considers how gender can be integrated. In this sense, the paper does not deviate from current literature – the overall goals for women's empowerment through the use of ICT policy are more or less universal. Examples of infoDev projects that relate to the policy areas are also presented for the purpose of illustration.

Define Laws and Policies

20

PAN Evaluations : Gender Integration and Policy Influence
International Development Research Centre (IDRC)
Neena Sachdeva; Dana Peebles. Kartini International. 2010

URL

http://idl-bnc.idrc.ca/dspace/handle/10625/45401

Purpose

To examine the extent to which PAN has pursued a systematic and appropriate approach to gender integration (or mainstreaming) and enhanced the level and quality of gender analysis into the research and applied research projects funded through PAN

Intended user

Gender advocates and Policy-makers

Available language(s)

English

Description

The paper examined the integration project-level gender integration within a selection of PAN projects, as well as the level of gender capacity and integration among the PAN team on a program-wide level. The evaluation used a utilization-focused participatory approach which involved all five core members of the PAN team in survey questionnaires, interviews and project review feedback. Each phase of the study was planned to engage the primary intended users and to inform the subsequent phases and analyses. The methodology included a combination of the Appreciative Inquiry methodology, and to some extent, the IDRC-funded Gender Evaluation Methodology (GEM) specifically created for ICT projects.

Define Laws and Policies

21

Trend and Status of Gender Perspectives in ICT Sector: Case Studies in Asia-Pacific Countries
International Telecommunication Union (ITU)
Sonam Wangmo; Sriyani Violina; Mozammel Haque. ITU. 2004

URL

http://unpan1.un.org/intradoc/groups/public/documents/apcity/unpan038243.pdf

Purpose

To know to what extent gender perspective is considered in ICT related policies, regulations, programs and activities run by government, international development partners and civil societies in Asia and the Pacific region.

Intended user

Governments, Policy-makers, Researchers and ICT Program planners

Available language(s)

English

Description

This report is based on a study conducted in three countries: Bangladesh, Bhutan and Indonesia during the period September-November 2004. The overall aim of this study is to find out the trend and status of gender in ICT from the case studies of three countries.

Establish Partnerships

22

Bridging the gender digital divide: A Report on Gender and ICT in Central Eastern Europe and the Commonwealth of Independent States

Fialova, K.; Simerska, L. UNDP&UNIFEM. 2005

URL

http://www.undp.org/content/dam/aplaws/publication/en/publications/poverty-reduction/poverty-website/bridging-the-gender-digital-divide/BridgingtheGenderDigitalDivide.pdf

Purpose

To know to what extent gender perspective is considered in ICT related policies, regulations, programs and activities run by government, international development partners and civil societies.

Intended user

Governments, Policy-makers, Researchers and ICT Program planners

Available language(s)

English

Description

The report focuses particularly on the integration of gender in relation to issues- such as access and control, education, training and skills development- which work towards achieving equal benefits from ICTs and their use to enhance opportunities for human development. A number of trends are identified specific to CEE/CIS, and other highlighted, which are global but are nevertheless of special importance for the region.

Conduct a Pilot Project

23

Toward Gender Equality in Europe and Eurasia: a Toolkit for Analysis
United States Agency for International Development (USAID)
Catherine Cozzarelli; Elisabeth Duban; JBS International. USAID. 2012

URL

http://www.gem2.org/sites/default/files/USAID_Gender_Equality_Toolkit%20for%20Analysis.pdf

Purpose

To provide programme staff with a resource for conducting gender analysis in the context of project design

Intended user

Governments, Policy-makers, Researchers and ICT Program planners

Available language(s)

English

Description

The Toolkit builds upon and supplements earlier initiatives, and provides concrete guidance and recommendations to assist in meeting USAID gender integration requirements. It is intended as a tool to assist in implementing USAID policy on promoting gender equality and female empowerment. The Toolkit provides an overview of the relevance of gender analysis to USAID development goals and uses the Six Domains Framework as a sample gender analysis methodology.

Conduct a Pilot Project

24

Gender and ICTs for Development: A Global Sourcebook

Royal Tropical Institute (KIT), The Netherlands & Oxfam GB

Minke Valk; S.J.R. Cummings; Henk Van Dam. KIT&Oxfam GB. 2005.

URL

http://www.unapcict.org/ecohub/resources/gender-and-icts-for-development-a-global-sourcebook

Purpose

To document the experiences of practitioners and experts in the South with respect to gender and ICTs in development

Intended user

Researchers and Practitioners

Available language(s)

English

Description

This book is a collection of case studies about women and their communities in developing countries, and how they have been influenced by ICTs. ICTs can have profound implications for women and men in terms of employment, education, health, environmental sustainability and community development.

Conduct a Pilot Project

25

E-government and Gender Digital Divide: The Case of Jordan

International Journal of Electronic Business Management (IJEBM)

Boran A. AL-Rababah; Emad A. Abu-Shanab. International Journal of Electronic Business Management. 2010; 8(1): 1-8

URL

http://ijebm.ie.nthu.edu.tw/IJEBM_Web/IJEBM_static/Paper-V8_N1/A01.pdf

Purpose

To suggest how the e-Government project in Jordan can empower poor women in rural areas with minimal or no ICT skills, and with no computers or Internet at their homes

Intended user

Practitioners, Researchers and Policy-makers

Available language(s)

English

Description

This research focuses on the future of e-Government empowerment roles for poor women and girls in developing countries based on realistic needs and strengthen by a suggested model to empower poor Jordanian women in rural areas by finding a link between what is already there in Jordan related to the initiatives that support this targeted group.

Annex B: Survey Questionnaires

Phase 1 (2011)

Aspects		Questionnaires	Type
Part 1. Demographic Information (4 questions)			
Respondent's basic information	1	Name,	Short answer
	2	email	Short answer
	3	Department/organization and country	Short answer
	4	Years of experience/ expert area	Short answer
Part II. ICT Policy for Women (10 questions)			
National level Policies - Gender & ICT	5	Is there a national strategy (including an implementation plan) or any initiative relating e-development for women - If "yes" please specify (link/doc)	Binary/ Web link
	6	National legal/ regulatory framework relating to e-development for women - If "yes" please specify	Binary/ Web link
	7-1	Relevant authority (department or ministry) in charge of national e- development program for women	Short answer
	7-2	Chief information officer (CIO) or a similar officer with a leadership role, to manage national e-development programs/ projects for women - If "yes" please specify	Binary/ Web link
	8	Are there specific projects / programs that are currently being undertaken under the National strategies specified above? - If "yes" please specify	Binary/ Link
	9-1	How **relevant is the objectives** of the projects/ programs in fulfilling the goals of the National strategy?	Scale
	9-2	How **well-formulated are the activities** of projects/ programs in fulfilling the goals of the National strategy?	Scale
	9-3	How **effective is the implementation** of the projects/ programs in fulfilling the goals of the National strategy?	Scale
Ministerial level Policies -Gender & ICT	10	Ministerial level strategy (including implementation plan) or any initiative relating to e-development for women - If "yes" please specify (link/doc)	Binary/ Web link
	11	Ministerial legal/ regulatory framework relating to e-development for women - If "yes" please specify	Binary/ Web link
	12-1	Relevant department/ division/office in charge of e- development program for women within ministry of gender	Short answer
	12-2	Chief information officer (CIO) or a similar officer with a leadership role, to manage e-development programs/ projects for women within the ministry of gender - If "yes" please specify	Binary/ Web link
	13	Are there specific projects / programs that are currently being undertaken under the Ministerial strategies specified above? - If "yes" please specify	Binary/ Link
	14-1	How **relevant is the objectives** of the projects/ programs in fulfilling the goals of the ministerial strategy?	Scale
	14-2	How **well-formulated are the activities** of projects/ programs in fulfilling the goals of the ministerial strategy?	Scale
	14-3	How **effective is the implementation** of the projects/ programs in fulfilling the goals of the ministerial strategy?	Scale

Effectiveness	15	What are the areas that need most **improvement** in the National Strategy (number in order of priority) - Relevancy of the objectives to solve problems - Feasibility of the project to achieve the goal - Effectiveness of implementation - Political will and commitment of the authority - Adequate level of human resources	Grid
	16	Has there been any significant achievement as a result of the above mentioned projects/ programs to promote women's ICT capacity building?	Short answer
	**Part III. Web Measurement of Ministry of Gender Site (33 questions)**
Information dissemination/ Outreach (Emerging State)	17	Existence of ministerial websites for ministry of gender equality or any institute performing equivalent functions - If "yes" please specify	Binary/ Web link
	18	Existence of a one-stop-shop portal for women - If "yes" please specify	Binary/ Web link
	19	Existence of an e-government section under the ministry website - If "yes" please specify	Binary/ Web link
	20	Sources of archived information (laws, policy documents, priorities, etc.)	Short answer
	21	News and/or updates on government policies relating to women	Short answer
	22	Access to back office applications (i.e. link to national e-government portal) - If "yes" please specify	Binary
	23	Information concerning government officials responsible for the provision of specific online services/queries for women - If "yes" please specify	Binary
	24	Personal account/profile of women, with the objective of enhancing dialogue between government and women - If "yes" please specify	Binary
	25	Information /contents - Please provide link/ documents	Short answer
	26*	Information for citizens/women on the usage of the website - If "yes" please specify	Binary/ Web link
Access/Usability (Enhanced Stage)	27	Search feature	Binary
	28	"Contact us" feature	Binary
	29	Audio and video features	Binary
	30	Multiple languages availability	Binary
	31	Use of wireless technology to send messages to mobile phones or devices - If "yes" please specify	Binary/ Web link
	32	Security (secure link) feature available/indicated	Binary
	33	Electronic signature feature	Binary
	34	Online payment by credit, debit, or other card methods	Binary
	35	E-mail sign-up option, either as a formal list-serv or simply for news items	Binary
	36	Existence of features to enable access for people with disabilities	Binary
Service Delivery Capability (Transactional Stage)	37	Downloadable/printable forms	Binary
	38	Online forms	Binary/
	39	Job opportunities	Binary
	40	Online transactions/ services available at the site - Please provide link/ documents	Short answer

	41	E-mail alerts for e-participation	Binary
	42	Really Simple Syndication (RSS) use for e-participation	Binary
	43	Set turnaround time for government to respond to submitted forms/e-mails	Binary
Citizen participation/ Interconnectedness (Connected Stage)	44	E-participation policy or mission statement - If "yes" please specify	Binary Web link
	45	Calendar listings of upcoming participatory activities	Binary
	46	Archived information about participatory activities	Binary
	47	Participatory tools to obtain public/women's opinion (polls, satisfaction surveys, bulletin boards, chat room, blogs, web casting, and discussion forums, social networking sites(SNS) etc.) - If "yes" please specify ※ May be provided in separate questions for each item	Binary/ Web link
	48	Provision for publishing the results of users feedback	Binary
	49	Archive on responses by government to citizen's questions, queries and inputs	Binary

Phase 2 (2012)

Questionnaire for Country Experts in Asia and the Pacific

Questionnaire for Country Experts in the Asia and Pacific

The emergence of information society has opened a new perspective on gender equality in public service, as many governments are exerting efforts to expand their public service outreach via government online portals and websites. However, there is also an increasing concern of women's exclusion from such online public service, due to the inequalities in access to Information and Communication Technology (ICT) and availability of online contents and services for women.

To respond to the growing call, **United Nations Project Office on Governance (UNPOG)** embarked on a research titled **"Role of e-Government to Promote Gender Equality in the Asia Pacific,"** which looked into the current status and future directions of ICT and e-Government development toward greater gender equality in six countries in the region.

This survey, conducted in part of the second phase of the UNPOG research, aims to collect opinions of experts in Asia and Pacific from a broad range of fields related to this increasingly crucial issue, including but not limited to gender development, social/public service and information communication technology.

Section Ⅰ. Respondent Information (Questions 1-4)

Section I. Respondent Information   UNPOG

*

1. Basic Information
Please provide your nationality and affiliation (required).
If you want to be contacted for further interview, please provided your name and email address.

*

2. Please check the type of your organization.

○   Governmental

○   Private

○   Academic

○   Other

*

3. Please check that best describes your area of expertise.

○   Gender development

○   Social service

○   ICT/ e-Government

○   Other

4. Would you like to be contacted for an in-depth interview and a country case study for this research?
If you answered "Yes" to this question, the research team will contact you via your email for a follow-up interview. Please make sure that you have provided a valid email address in question 1.

○   Yes

○   No

Section II. Gender Equality and ICT/e-Government Development (Questions 5-12)

5. Is there a national policy, strategy (including an implementation plan) or any initiative relating to <u>ICT development for women</u>?
In this context, "ICT development for women" refers to the general use of information and communication technology (ICT) for women's empowerment.

○ Yes

○ No

6. If you answered "Yes" to the previous question, please provide details of the policy, including the title, government agency in charge of the policy, and brief summary of the contents.
If available, please provide the URL link and/or documentation. Documentation should be emailed to apwinc@sm.ac.kr .

[text box]

*

7. In your opinion, which entity has currently the strongest <u>influence and ownership</u> over policies relating to ICT development for women?
Please rank in order of greatest influence, i.e. the strongest influence: 1, the least influence: 7

[▼] Ministry (Department) of ICT or equivalent

[▼] Ministry (Department) of Gender development or equivalent

[▼] Ministry (Department) of Social service or equivalent

[▼] Other Central agency (i.e. President/ Prime Minister's Office, Central Party, etc.)

[▼] Private ICT sector

[▼] Other NGOs/ Academia in gender area

[▼] Other NGOs/ Academia in ICT area

8. To what extent the following <u>objectives</u> have importance in the national ICT development policies for women?

	Not Important	Slightly Important	Average	Important	Very Important
Improve women's access to ICT	○	○	○	○	○
Enhance women's ICT capacity	○	○	○	○	○
Collect information on women's ICT needs and usage	○	○	○	○	○
Integrate gender concerns into national ICT policies	◉	○	○	○	○
Ensure women's equal opportunities in accessing public services	○	○	○	○	○
Promote women's participation in public decision-making process	◉	○	○	○	○

147

	Not Important	Slightly Important	Average	Important	Very Important
Develop e-Government services for women	○	○	○	○	○
Build women's online communities and networks	○	○	○	○	○
Encourage private sector to develop ICT applications and services for women	○	○	○	○	○
Advocate the importance of women's online participation in public sector	○	○	○	○	○

9. Please evaluate the following statements regarding the <u>impact</u> of national ICT development policies for women.

	Strongly Disagree	Disagree	Neutral	Agree	Strongly Agree
The policy has improved women's access to information on government services.	○	○	○	○	○
The policy has promoted women's participation in political and democratic process.	○	○	○	○	○
The policy has captured women's needs/ demands of ICT and e-government services.	○	○	○	○	○
The policy has supported women parliamentarians.	○	○	○	○	○
The policy has contributed to improve the online service quality of Ministry of Gender.	○	○	○	○	○
The policy has delivered online social services for women. (i.e. e-learning, e-health)	○	○	○	○	○
Overall, the policy has contributed to enhance gender equality in public sector.	○	○	○	○	○

10. What are the <u>two</u> most important areas where more policy efforts are needed in your country in order to promote e-Government development for women? <u>(Please select two)</u>

☐ Identify women's ICT and e-government service needs

☐ Collect gender-disaggregated national statistics on ICT

☐ Design e-government and ICT-enabled public services reflecting women's needs

☐ Improve delivery of e-government and ICT-enabled public services for women

☐ Develop institutional/ staff capacity to carry out e-government programs and services

☐ Strengthen the inter-connectedness between women's e-development and national ICT / e-government strat

☐ Monitor the gender impacts of e-government services for women

☐ Build alliance with private / non-governmental sector for partnership

☐ Other (Please specify)

11. Please rate the importance of addressing the following <u>obstacles</u> to promote e-Government service development for women in your country.

	Not Important	Slightly Important	Average	Important	Very Important
Income inequality between women and men	○	○	○	○	○
Language barrier	○	○	○	○	○
Lack of local contents and information relevancy reflecting women's needs	○	○	○	○	○
Different gender patterns of technology use	○	○	○	○	○
Attitudes of women towards technology	○	○	○	○	○
Lack of national data/statistics on women's ICT usage	○	○	○	○	○
Lack of gender analysis in the telecommunication industry	○	○	○	○	○
Lack of government staff's expertise in ICT	○	○	○	○	○
Lack of gender-friendly framework in public administration	○	○	○	○	○
Lack of inter-agency coordination across the government	○	○	○	○	○

*

12. In your opinion, which entity should play a <u>leadership</u> role in the e-Government development policies for women in your country?
Please rank in order of importance, i.e. the most important: 1, the least important: 5.

[▼] Ministry (Department) of ICT or equivalent

[▼] Ministry (Department) of Gender development or equivalent

[▼] Central government agency (i.e. President/ Prime Minister's Office, Central Party, etc.)

[▼] Private ICT sector

[▼] Other NGOs/ Academia

Section III. UN e-Government Survey (Questions 13-17)

The Global E-Government Development Reports and Survey are initiatives led by UN Department of Economic and Social Affairs (DESA) Division of Public Administration and Development Management (DPADM), which present a systemic assessment of how governments use Information and Communications Technology (ICT) to provide access and inclusion for all.

To arrive at a set of online service index value of the Report, the researchers assess each country's national website, including the national central portal, e-services portal and e-participation portal, as well as the websites of the related ministries of education, labour, social services, health, finance, and environment as applicable. In this index, currently, <u>the national website of ministry of gender development or equivalent is **not** included</u> .

For more information, please visit <u>here</u> .

*

13. In order to adequately reflect <u>gender equality criteria to the UN e-Government Survey</u>, how important do you think are the following tasks?

	Not Important	Slightly Important	Average	Important	Very Important
Include website analysis of Ministry of Gender or equivalent to online service quality assessment.	○	○	○	○	○
Use gender-disaggregated national ICT statistics for assessment.	○	○	○	○	○
Develop a toolkit to facilitate collection of women's e-Government usage data at national level.	○	○	○	○	○
Develop a new sub-index which looks at the gender gap in e-Government outreach.	○	○	○	○	○

Other (Please specify)

*

14. Currently in your country, are gender-disaggregated ICT statistics available?

○ Yes

○ No

○ Other (Please specify)

15. Please suggest <u>one national website in your country</u> that is directly related to gender development (i.e. website of Ministry of Gender or equivalent), which you believe is <u>most appropriate for the UN e-Government Survey analysis in gender equality criteria</u>. Please provide the name and URL link of the website.